PURSUIT
OF
EXCELLENCE

Building Your Leadership Foundation

PURSUIT
OF
EXCELLENCE

H. MARC HELM

STRONGPrint
PUBLISHING

Visit the author's website at marchelm.com

STRONGPrint Publishing
Windsor, CO

Helm, H. Marc
Pursuit of Excellence
Building Your Leadership Foundation

Library of Congress Control Number: 2024902802
Pursuit of Excellence: Building Your Leadership Foundation
ISBN: 978-1-962074-17-9 (paperbook)
ISBN: 978-1-962074-18-6 (ebook)

DEDICATION

To my lovely, exceptionally educated daughter, Jean Ann Helm Allen. I dedicate the essence of this book to you, as your life and achievements have inspired me to share thoughts and experiences with others and hopefully make a difference.

CONTENTS

INTRODUCTION

"A leader is one who knows the way, goes the
way and shows the way."

JOHN MAXWELL

In my forty-five-plus years of experience in business, I have grown to truly understand the difference between what it takes to become a successful leader versus a successful manager. Leadership and management are two distinct but interconnected concepts, both of which play a critical role in the success of any organization. A leader could be a successful manager, and a manager could evolve into a successful leader, but it is quite possible for someone to only be good at one of the two roles. Leaders prioritize employees and relationships, while managers prioritize tasks and processes. Leaders often have a long-term perspective, while managers focus on short-term results. Leaders tend to be more innovative, while managers are more systematic.

Leadership involves inspiring and motivating employees or members to work toward a common vision or goal. A leader inspires and influences employees or a defined group of individuals to work towards a shared goal by providing direction, guidance, and support. Successful leaders possess excellent communication skills, emotional intelligence, and a strong sense of purpose. They are passionate visionaries who lead by example, understand their team members' strengths and weaknesses, and know how to leverage these human assets to achieve collective goals and successes.

Management involves the process of planning, organizing, directing, and controlling resources to achieve organizational goals. Successful managers possess strong analytical skills, decision-making abilities, and excellent problem-solving skills. They are also efficient, organized, and ensure projects and tasks are completed on track and within budget. However, we must realize that as management and their teams focus on specific goals, they have to be effective at communicating and executing the vision to their staff members.

Despite these differences, both leaders and managers are critical for the overall success of an organization. Leadership and management need to work together to ensure the organization achieves its goals efficiently and effectively. For instance, while leaders may have a vision, managers ensure the vision is translated into action through planning, organizing, directing, and controlling resources. Leaders must inspire employees to adhere to and achieve a common goal, while managers provide the necessary resources and support to achieve the goal.

Both leadership and management are therefore necessary for the overall success of an organization. A balance of leadership and management skills is essential to drive the organization toward long-term success, and hopefully ensure we have talented leaders and managers to follow in our footsteps – a daunting challenge but certainly an achievable one. The first step to putting this process into action is to recognize these differences. The leader is the visionary, the inspiration, the one who is taking challenges and successes to a high enough level to be dealt with, and the one who takes ownership of a company. They may be looking at how supply and demand impact their market or how the political climate is impacting their industry. A manager's goal is to produce the best quality product or provide the best quality service to the customer in the quickest and most cost-effective manner while maintaining high-quality customer service and addressing issues and challenges as they may arise.

What separates a bad leader from a competent leader is their sincerity in appreciating when an employee or manager comes to them with a quicker, better, or faster way of doing something. A good leader will appreciate that knowledge and let that person know they are indispensable to the organization. Nothing would make me happier than helping to bring out the best leader in each one of you.

CHAPTER 1

LEADERS ARE MADE, NOT BORN

"Lead, follow, or get out of the way."

GEORGE PATTON

Contrary to popular belief, leaders are made, not born. For centuries, we viewed leadership as genetic, thinking certain families or dynasties were predisposed to becoming successful leaders. But this doesn't mean it's all predetermined—there is always potential for anyone to become a competent and inspirational leader with hard work and dedication. Being a leader is much more than just having an authoritative title. True leaders have charisma that sets them apart from others in the same type of position. While anybody can be trained in leadership, qualities like strong ethics or a knack for problem-solving are unique to each individual.

When someone is born into a leadership role, it can be a recipe for disaster. There is often an assumption that their job is bestowed upon them, creating entitlement, which isn't a good approach to running a business. I've seen this play out in the corporate world more times than I'd like to recount, where the sons or brothers of the founder take on a leadership position with little to no experience. While they may have gone through some sort of rite of passage, it doesn't mean they know what they're doing, and sometimes that sense of entitlement takes over, leading them to believe they are infallible and their decisions are always right.

As history proves time and time again, no one is above or immune from making mistakes. These mistakes are often lessons best learned sooner rather than later. Too often, this "entitlement" is seen as an excuse for poor behavior or management. Having experienced many of these situations firsthand in some form or another, where there's an unspoken expectation that someone has earned their leadership position, I can empathize. There is an unfortunate arrogance that comes along with that style, and they may believe they don't have to justify their decisions. This makes those around them feel uncomfortable when attempting to voice any disagreement and leaves many walking on eggshells, not wanting to risk confrontation.

The assertion that great leaders are born overlooks the fact that everyone, regardless of their birth circumstances, can take responsibility for their development. Those who rise to leadership positions develop both knowledge and experience in the areas they manage while honing the skills to lead others through communication, decision-making, problem-solving, and the implementation of ideas. Ineffective and effective leaders have one thing in common—they all make mistakes—but how these mistakes are confronted and resolved is what sets an effective leader apart from a poor one. Making a commitment to continually invest in learning how to be an excellent leader will help anyone achieve that goal.

A Leader Does Not Need a Leadership Position

Leadership is so much more than just having a title or holding a specific position. It is about having the ability to inspire and motivate others, build trust, have a vision, and the ability to turn ideas into reality. Anyone can be a leader with the proper development. Although Mahatma Gandhi did not hold any specific office or title, he was able to lead millions of people in India's struggle for independence from British rule. Though small in stature and lacking resources, he had the courage and conviction to make change happen with his leadership abilities. He was able to influence millions of people through his commitment to nonviolence, justice, and truth.

Any person can show effective leadership skills by standing out from the crowd through active listening, understanding what motivates their team, creating an inclusive environment, setting standards for quality performance, and holding space for constructive dialogue around project execution. Anyone blessed with these skills has the potential to rise as a leader.

In today's business world, many employees across organizations have become more engaged in their jobs when it comes to making decisions and giving feedback on the processes necessary to execute tasks. Technology has increased transparency in organizations and enables greater collaboration opportunities, so everyone has an equal say in the success or failure of projects, regardless of whether they are supervisors or team members at lower-level positions in the company's hierarchy. This means anyone who dares take the initiative could become a leader by taking on responsibilities beyond their job descriptions and focusing on a larger mission rather than their short-term objectives. When companies encourage this sort of initiative, it unleashes innovative potential among employees while impacting the bottom line positively for the organization overall, further creating a unique competitive edge in comparison to those without such empowering cultures.

Steve Jobs is considered one of the best leaders in business culture, not because of a title, but due to his passion for innovation and customer experience, which made Apple products the worldwide standard they are today. Despite being fired from Apple as CEO, Jobs returned years later as interim CEO and revived the company by introducing revolutionary products such as the iPod, iPhone, and iPad, which transformed how we live our daily lives. Great leadership can come from someone outside traditional corporate structures because it relies on vision, strength, and the capability to execute plans with teams rather than working alone from a top-down approach.

Evolving Into a Leader

As a leader, your situation and environment will determine what kind of leader you can be. Being aware of this can help you maneuver through difficult situations more gracefully and confidently. If you desire to become an effective leader, you need to assess the context and react accordingly. It is entirely up to each individual leader to decide how proactive they need to be to find success in any given space.

Success in leadership isn't a one-time achievement—it's an ongoing process. Being a leader is all about learning how to constantly adapt and maintain success in your own life, as well as in the lives of those around you. Everyone will eventually face times when they are called upon to lead, no matter what profession or sector they work in. Growing into a successful leader requires training, focus, commitment, and dedication—but with the right guidance, anyone can learn how to take charge of their destiny confidently and effectively. Here is what it takes to evolve into an influential leader that inspires greatness amongst their peers. As you read each of these elements, think about how leaders throughout history, pop culture, and your life have been created from these key elements.

DESIRE

Leadership is not a position; it is a mindset. If you aim to be a leader, you must first have that inner desire to lead. It cannot be forced upon you, nor can it be learned from a textbook. The qualities that make a great leader, such as confidence, empathy, and the ability to inspire, come from within. It is only when you truly believe in yourself and your vision that you can inspire others to follow you. As I always say, "If your actions inspire others to dream more, learn more, do more, and become more, you are better postured to be an effective leader." So, if you have that inner fire to lead, let it burn brightly and watch as others follow in your footsteps.

VISION & CLARITY

Leadership requires foresight and imagination, and both of these qualities can be encapsulated in one central concept—vision. A clear, compelling vision is essential for any leader who hopes to inspire and motivate their team to achieve greatness. Vision is the guiding light that gives direction and purpose to all of a leader's actions and decisions. Without vision, leaders risk wandering aimlessly without a sense of direction. A leader who has a strong vision can rally their team behind a cause and inspire everyone to work together to make that vision a reality. A leader without a vision is like a ship without a rudder—they may still move forward, but they are far more likely to be blown off course by the winds of circumstance.

Without a vision and clarity, followers will struggle to align their efforts toward a common goal. In war, leaders must make crucial decisions that can turn the tides of the battle, so they need to make sure their decisions align with the vision for the war. Whether you agree with war or not, no one fights a war for no reason—there is always a purpose and a vision behind it. A good leader will run ideas by others who can poke holes in their thought process to come to the best decision overall. Though General Robert E. Lee was a great strategist, he made the worst possible decision in the Battle of Gettysburg by sending the Confederate soldiers across the field into the barrage of artillery. In this case, Lee didn't have a good set of advisors like he had before. He lost Stonewall Jackson, and George Pickett was an egomaniac who convinced Lee the charge was a good idea.

Similarly, in any industry, leaders are essential for innovation and progress. Effective leaders possess the vision, skills, and knowledge to implement plans and guide their teams toward success. They facilitate and support the efforts of the team by promoting collaboration and teamwork, which is essential to accomplish the mission. By providing a level of clarity and setting expectations right from the start, leaders can build a team of strong, effective individuals who can take our business to the next level. If you aspire to be a leader, start by developing a clear and compelling vision for yourself and your organization.

CONFRONT

Leadership results from the overall efforts of an individual and their capacity to question the established order so positive change can be achieved. Unfortunately, it's all too common for people to handle this process in a negative way. When confronting someone with the intention to make effective solutions, leaders need to involve the person being challenged instead of confronting them directly. This will drive collaboration and engagement as they feel they are part of the decision-making process rather than feeling attacked, threatened, or like a victim of the process.

Leadership can be difficult, especially when you have someone in a position of power who may not recognize the value you can bring to the table. This happens often in family-owned businesses where leadership roles are given based on familial relationships. While this is challenging, it is important to remember that no matter your circumstances, there are always ways to work together and create positive outcomes. When confronting someone in a leadership position, it is important to approach the situation with respect. Make sure the person knows you value their opinion and experience while at the same time presenting your own ideas for how things could be done differently to be quicker, better, or faster. Don't come off as confrontational or cocky. Instead, truly try to work together with them on solutions and strategies moving forward.

Always keep an open mind and stay flexible, but don't get so distracted that your voice or ideas go unheard. Working with someone who has never been confronted before requires patience, and both sides should always engage with respect. Showing them there are other ways of doing things that don't compromise their overall goals is key to finding common ground.

At all times, when working with any leader, it's important to remember that success requires teamwork and a willingness to learn from each other—regardless of one's upbringing, personal history, or professional experience. By providing honest feedback without arrogance and recognizing one another's strengths without coming off as overbearing, true leadership comes alive between two individuals who are more willing than ever before to take on any challenges ahead of them.

VALUABLE CRITICISM

Have you ever received criticism and immediately felt defensive or even hurt? I think we have all been there. However, it's important to remember criticism can be incredibly valuable, even if it may not initially seem so. As a leader, giving criticism can be nerve-wracking.

You want to make sure your team understands your intention is constructive, not to hurt or offend anyone. Here are the three ways in which criticism can be valuable in an organization:

- Providing perspective: Criticism can change the current way someone is viewing something or open their eyes up to other options they may not have seen before. When giving criticism to provide a new perspective, make sure the other person understands you intend to help them grow with feedback. Positive encouragement and focusing on the issue at hand go a long way in improving interpersonal relationships and effective communication within the workplace.

- Streamlining processes, creating better products, and optimizing business practices: Criticism can offer insight and understanding into issues that could be causing trouble for customers or employees. If something isn't making money or is more costly than budgeted for, criticism and suggestions can help course-correct those issues. In addition to monetary gains, this can be incredibly helpful in improving employee morale regarding the quality of the product. If staff members have not been performing as efficiently as they should be, considering their ideas can go a long way towards revamping that product, thus making everyone feel proud of the output they fostered.

- Innovation: Criticism can push boundaries and transform something good into something great, whether it's reducing costs or creating a product one step above anyone else's. It can be as simple as offering suggestions to see how someone will react or as complex as giving them explicit ideas to reduce costs and create something new. The point is to support growth and productivity in whatever way possible while still being considerate of the feelings of those it may impact. By advocating for better products, better safety protocols, and improved efficiency, constructive criticism can help sustain a positive difference in any situation.

A bicycle shop owner in Houston, Texas had an interesting experience when one of his workers took a test ride on one of their bikes. The bike was a high-end racing model, and the worker was maintaining some decent speed. However, when the worker applied the brakes, he noticed a slight delay before coming to a stop. The owner knew this could be dangerous, as riders need to make last-minute adjustments while passing other racers. After looking into the problem together, they realized the issue was in how the brake line was situated. It wasn't bent correctly and thus slowed down reaction time. After making corrections to the brake line, the bike started working perfectly and was able to stop without delay. By listening to criticism and making constructive recommendations, they were able to improve their product. Not only did they avoid any potential disasters, but they also received positive reviews due to their efforts, which is always great for business.

Through this story, we can draw some important lessons around criticism:

- It's important to listen to criticism and incorporate feedback into our products.

- Don't hesitate to collaborate with others who have more knowledge or experience.

- Examine products or services carefully for any signs of weaknesses or flaws—small adjustments can have big impacts.

- Vital information may come from unexpected places, so always aim for continuous improvement of your products and services.

Great leaders know criticism is a source of value, not something to be dreaded. They understand the importance of listening to each situation and coming up with compromises that work for both sides. When done well, criticism can become something staff members appreciate hearing, recognizing the person giving it as someone who truly cares about their development.

Valuable criticism separates a good leader from the rest because they can analyze situations with an objective eye and deliver constructive feedback in a way that provides direction without offending or belittling. A leader should always strive to provide useful criticism, not one that lands flat or is overly harsh. This shows respect for the team and encourages open dialogue about areas of improvement. However, as with everything in life, there needs to be a balance between providing effective feedback and ensuring the team remains motivated and engaged with the task at hand. This will help build trust and loyalty, which will be beneficial for the long-term growth of the company.

EXECUTE

Have you ever felt like your team is constantly busy but not actually getting things done? It could be that they're taking action, but not executing. While these may sound like interchangeable terms, there is a crucial difference. Taking action is just that—doing something. It could be a small response to a problem or a grand idea for the future, but it doesn't necessarily mean progress is being made. Taking action can be thought of as an initiative or effort to make something happen, such as starting a project or introducing a new product. There is no specific plan laid out, and it involves proactivity rather than following set instructions.

Execution, on the other hand, is about following through and achieving goals. It involves the completion of a plan from beginning to end, starting with the development and research stages, progressing to implementation, and finally culminating in evaluation. Execution involves careful planning as well as assessing progress along the way, with mistakes being corrected if necessary. Anyone can take action, but successful leaders execute effectively.

The execution process involves recognizing the importance of each step and ensuring they are all completed with equal importance. If you are coaching someone and giving them suggestions on how to improve, they must execute every aspect of the plan. Skipping steps could lead to failure, and it's essential to recognize every step in the execution process is vital to success. In other words, execution is not just about getting things done but about getting them done correctly.

Many times, we tend to overcomplicate our tasks and processes, whether it's in business or our daily lives. We may find ourselves in situations where people do not want to listen or follow through with the actions needed. However, executing is the only way to see results. By being decisive and executing, leaders can move forward toward their goals and objectives.

It's important to recognize that not everyone has the same level of knowledge or expertise on a subject, and assumptions should not be made. Successful execution takes into consideration the quality of the product, relations with employees, and deliverability to the intended audience. Therefore, understanding the power of proper execution and its effects is crucial for leaders.

A TWO-WAY PHENOMENON

Becoming a leader is more than just leading a team. It's about understanding that leadership is a two-way phenomenon. When you empower your team to grow and develop their leadership skills, everyone benefits. They become better able to take charge and make decisions, ultimately making your job easier. Remember, leadership is not about controlling others but rather working collaboratively and inspiring one another to achieve a common goal. So if you want to be a successful leader, remember your success is dependent on the success of those around you. I always tell my team that if they want me to be a good leader, they need to be good leaders themselves.

SELF-ACTUALIZE

Self-actualization is a new concept that has come up in psychology in the last 30 years or so. It's a concept of the mind, where you feel a sense of peace and comfort in yourself and what you are doing. This isn't something that can be determined or evaluated by other people—it comes from within. Self-actualization doesn't mean you feel completely comfortable with all facets of your life, but it's a feeling you get with specific aspects of who you are and what you are capable of.

If becoming a leader in your organization is your goal, achieving self-actualization is a crucial step on the journey. In business, self-actualization refers to the process of fulfilling your potential as a person and achieving a job-related sense of personal fulfillment. Leaders who have achieved self-actualization are often able to inspire others to grow and reach their potential. They lead with confidence, passion, and a deep understanding of their strengths and weaknesses. Achieving self-actualization requires self-awareness, a willingness to learn and grow, and a commitment to personal development. It may take time and effort, but the rewards of becoming a self-actualized leader are immense. By focusing on your growth and development, you can become the kind of leader who inspires those around you to reach their potential.

It's easy to fall into the trap of thinking you are invincible or a god of some sort. You may have moments where you think this way, but it is important to recognize that everyone, including yourself, is fallible and can make mistakes. To help yourself from getting lost in the proverbial wilderness, having a sense of direction and using tools as guides can be incredibly helpful. When you instill these key points within yourself and build upon them over time, it will become easier for someone else to look up to you and become inspired by your leadership qualities.

To reach a level of leadership and esteem amongst others, start to practice self-reflection and discipline regularly. Track your progress by setting goals that are realistic yet challenging enough so they require effort on your part. Take the time to listen carefully and acknowledge the advice of others since ideas from diverse sources can help you find solutions faster. Last but not least, don't be afraid to take risks while at the same time minimizing potential losses by formulating plans with several alternatives in mind.

Once you have built strong foundations for yourself through hard work and perseverance, turn your focus outward towards those around you and share what you have learned. Your self-actualization will inspire greatness in others with kindness rather than force. After all, true leaders motivate others without being too authoritative. As long as you stay humble yet confident in your skillset, success will follow suit quickly thereafter.

Lead, Follow, or Get Out of the Way

The military is a place where discipline and leadership are essential qualities. In the army, there's an expression that encapsulates these qualities: "Lead, follow, or get the hell out of the way." To be a leader, you don't just need to give orders; you need to help those around you and be a motivator. On the other hand, to be a follower, it's not enough just to follow; you need to support the leader and be a team player. However, if you can't lead or follow effectively, then you should get out of the way because the world won't wait for you. This expression is so applicable that it's even written on a gate at the United States Army Infantry School at Fort Benning, Georgia. Overall, "lead, follow, or get the hell out of the way" is a fitting reminder that everyone has a role to play, and we all need to do our part.

Part of a leader's responsibility is to get everyone on the same page. If you have a company with over 100 employees from a Vice President to a receptionist, you need to make sure everyone understands what you are trying to accomplish so they can assist you in getting there. If someone is just going to get in the way or get in the way of other people accomplishing their part of the job, then they need to get out of the way. I've seen this happen more times than I can count, where one person does not have 100% buy-in and they derail the whole process.

In one of my companies, we focused on streamlining our approval process for the assumptions on mortgage loans. We had an underwriter who looked at the package and came up with suggestions on conditions that needed to be cured to be approved. What happened was we had a manager who let his knowledgeable underwriting person go in an attempt to save money, which resulted in our entire process failing. We then had to work backward, and anytime you must work backward in business, it's not efficient. In this case, we had a manager who we thought understood the process after we changed the process, but he eliminated one of the core control points of the process, which caused the overall process to fail.

As leaders, we need to lay the process out in a way that emphasizes its importance. If you can't be a leader or a follower, then you simply need to get out of the way because you could be detrimental to the process or the company at large.

Breaking Boundaries to Become a Leader

Leadership can be acquired through experience, learning, and perseverance. But we cannot deny that some people are born with certain privileges that can greatly aid them in their journey toward leadership. Privilege can come in many forms, such as financial stability, access to education, or even innate charisma. While privilege alone does not make a leader, it can certainly provide opportunities and advantages less privileged individuals may not have. It is important to acknowledge the role privilege can play in leadership and work towards creating a more inclusive and equal society where everyone has the same opportunities to become a leader.

Becoming a leader can often feel like an uphill battle, especially for those who come from low-income families. For some, like myself, when surrounded by supportive and loving parents, anything is possible. Despite their struggles, my parents made it their mission to give me every opportunity to succeed. They believed in me, encouraged me, and instilled a strong sense of self-worth in me. Through their unwavering dedication, they were able to provide me with the tools and knowledge needed to navigate the often challenging road to success. Today, I am grateful for the opportunities they provided and proud of all I have accomplished with their support. But again, it goes to show how having some sort of opportunity in life, whether financial or emotional, can have a great impact on where you end up in life.

Life can be tough. For some, the road to success is paved with opportunities waiting to be taken. For others, it's a long journey with no end in sight. Some may be lucky enough to have opportunities handed to them on a silver platter, while others have to fight tooth and nail just to be seen and heard. It's heartbreaking to think so many potential leaders are stifled by circumstance—their dreams and ambitions dashed before they even have a chance to start. From inadequate education and limited resources to discrimination and bias, there are countless obstacles standing in the way of those striving to become leaders. The emotional toll of being constantly overlooked and undervalued is immeasurable, but through it all, these individuals persevere. They refuse to be defeated by their circumstances, and they are the epitome of strength and resilience.

Alexander the Great is one of the most well-known historical figures. He is largely remembered for his unparalleled conquests and his unyielding leadership that made him one of the greatest military commanders of all time. Despite dying in his thirties, Alexander had already accomplished more than many individuals today do in their much longer lives. He was relentless in his pursuit of power and never gave up, even when faced with seemingly insurmountable obstacles. But it's important to remember Alexander came from a privileged family and had access to opportunities that many others did not. Whether you like to admit it or not, leadership can sometimes be born from opportunities—but that doesn't guarantee anyone will be a good leader.

While some people may be born with certain privileges that can assist them to become leaders, ultimately, it is their dedication, hard work, and resilience that truly set them apart. Privilege can certainly provide advantages, such as access to resources and opportunities, but it cannot guarantee success in leadership. It is important to acknowledge and address inequities and biases that may exist in our society, but we should not discredit the hard work and determination of individuals who have achieved success through their own efforts. Ultimately, leadership is about taking initiative, making difficult decisions, and motivating others towards a common goal, regardless of background or privilege.

One of the most fulfilling experiences of my life has been working with underprivileged youth and watching them achieve their goals and dreams. These individuals understand the value of hard work and determination, and they have a drive to succeed that cannot be matched. I firmly believe a person's race or socioeconomic background should not limit their potential for success. It's time for us to recognize everyone deserves a chance to thrive, regardless of the circumstances they were born into. As a leader, you have to uplift and empower those who may have faced challenging times so they, too, can accomplish their biggest dreams.

Outsourcing in India was an eye-opening experience for me. As I managed the process for a large bank, I couldn't help but notice the pervasive caste system in India. It was disheartening to see how people were discriminated against based on the family they were born into. However, amidst all the inequality, I was inspired by the way some people managed to break free from the shackles of their caste and rise above it. Education played a crucial role in their journey to upward mobility.

Because the caste system in India limited opportunities, many people in the lower castes decided to work for outsourcers, which are companies that hire others to do their work for them, and, in many cases, these people are from other countries. Many of those outsourcers opted to pay for their education, which was an opportunity for them to move beyond their caste. This strategy involved getting an education while actively working and using the acquired skills to advance in their career. Once individuals gained the necessary knowledge and expertise, they broke out on their own or pursued their career goals elsewhere. This included starting a business or immigrating to a location with greater prospects for growth and success. For those with ambition and drive, this approach offered a pathway to personal and professional advancement. It was heartwarming to see how some were able to access education and go on to make their mark in fields like medicine, law, and business. Many of them ended up in the United States, pursuing their dreams and chasing life's opportunities.

Opportunities are what we strive for to succeed in life, but the mindset of the individual also plays a crucial role in determining their success. You are not limited by your circumstances, whether it be your place of birth or difficult personal experiences. It's important to remember these things may be challenging, but they aren't roadblocks and should never be used as an excuse for not achieving your self-actualization. Your success is not predetermined by external factors, but it is based on your determination to overcome obstacles and achieve your goals. Whether you come from a war-torn country or have a difficult upbringing, know that you are capable of accomplishing great things.

Through commitment, hard work, and a willingness to learn, anyone can develop the skills needed to lead effectively. The journey toward becoming a great leader begins with self-awareness and a commitment to personal growth. It involves learning to communicate effectively, making tough decisions, empowering others, and inspiring a shared vision. While some may have a natural inclination towards leadership, it is the willingness to learn and grow that truly sets successful leaders apart.

THOUGHT MANAGEMENT

- How can leaders effectively confront their team members when providing criticism for improvement without creating a hostile environment?
- What strategies can leaders use to develop a clear and compelling vision for their organization?
- In what ways can leaders balance executing plans effectively while also empowering their team members to take on responsibilities beyond their job descriptions?
- How can leaders recognize and address privilege within their organizations to create a more inclusive and equitable environment for aspiring leaders?

CHAPTER 2

CHARACTERISTICS OF A SUCCESSFUL LEADER

"The art of communication is the language of leaders."

JAMES HUMES

Whether they are recognized by a company with a formal job title and accompanying salary or simply viewed as a leader amongst their peers, leaders are expected to be actively involved in an organization's processes and observe how employees interact with customers and handle tasks. By doing so, they can identify potential problems or bottlenecks in the process and take corrective action before minor issues become major obstacles. Leaders should lead by example and demonstrate the behavior they expect from their employees to create a supportive work environment. By instilling self-worth in their team, leaders can empower them to take ownership of their tasks and feel valued in their roles. When employees feel valued, they are more likely to perform at their best, which ultimately leads to better end products and customer satisfaction.

By actively overseeing the process, leading by example, instilling self-worth in employees, and providing effective feedback, leaders can ensure processes run smoothly and their end products meet or exceed expectations. Leaders must strike a balance between managing the process and managing their employees, creating a work environment that fosters growth, development, satisfied customers, improved product quality, and a more productive and engaged workforce.

Communication

Successful leaders excel in effective communication, and I would argue this is the most important characteristic of a successful leader. Without the ability to deliver a message effectively, neither you nor the individuals you are leading will be able to accomplish anything. If your team is not on the same page or their feelings are overlooked, projects can quickly fail. So, it is important to ensure your team can comprehend, act upon, and embrace your message.

The way you communicate reflects on your credibility and professionalism and the company's capability to serve potential customers, employees, or partners. Taking the time to properly craft and develop a message can not only ensure your point is made but also acts as a representation of your company as a whole. Strong written and verbal communication helps build trust with all your stakeholders by demonstrating an understanding of their needs and expectations— something that should be maintained with every interaction, which can make or break the overall opinion of a company. Doing this is essential to creating a positive reputation to enable the growth of your company.

Successful leaders understand how their behavior influences those around them and use communication to build bridges with their team to create relationships based on trust and understanding. Using effective, open communication allows leaders to create an environment where team members feel comfortable speaking up about any issues they may be facing, while simultaneously ensuring conversations always remain professional. Leaders should leverage their authority and demonstrate respect for colleagues when discussing any difficult topics, demonstrating empathy rather than judgment when appropriate.

Part of communication is understanding who your audience is, whether it's your boss, your team, or a large group of industry professionals. Gaining a deep understanding of your audience allows you to tailor your content and delivery method to effectively communicate your intended message. Factors to consider while understanding your audience include their interests, educational backgrounds, cultural values, and potential questions or concerns they may have. With this information, you can create content and use language that resonates with them, forming a deeper connection and making your conversation more impactful.

Whenever you communicate with your team, your words do not simply vanish after the meeting ends. Consider what sort of message you would like your audience to take home with them or apply in their daily lives. Prepare powerful phrases and anecdotes that will stay in their minds long enough for them to comprehend your message and apply it when needed. Whether it's a directive or a thought-provoking comment, consider what you want the person or people you are speaking with to take away from the conversation.

When engaging in open communication, here are some components to keep in mind:

- Clear and concise language: Leaders should avoid jargon or long-winded explanations when possible, focusing instead on giving straightforward instructions or asking direct questions. This process reduces the chances of misinterpretations or misunderstandings between parties, which can lead to conflict and frustration further down the line.

- Active listening: This involves taking the time to truly listen without interruption and repeating back what has been said to confirm understanding. By engaging in active listening, leaders can ensure they understand what their team members are saying before responding or making decisions. This helps build trust with team members, as it shows the leader is taking them seriously.

- Invite participation: Engaging with others allows us to share different perspectives and gain new insights on a wide range of subjects. This can sometimes feel challenging if you're giving a presentation, but it's still possible through interactivity. Without the participation of the people you are speaking with, an essential aspect of dialogue is lost. For those who choose not to participate, it is important to remind them their ideas and opinions still matter. If they are not comfortable enough to speak up at the time, let them know they can bring their thoughts up with their supervisor or manager later on. Each person's contributions are valuable in achieving the goals set out for their department as a whole, and the voices of everyone involved have a meaningful impact on each individual's success.

- Feedback: Leaders should provide frequent feedback on how employees are progressing so everyone knows exactly where they stand in terms of performance and individual strengths can be identified and nurtured. Feedback should be specific, timely, and actionable to enable employees to improve their performance. It should be delivered constructively and respectfully to promote a growth mindset, encourage performance improvement, and foster a culture of continuous learning.

- Implementation: To show you have truly heard what the other person is communicating to you, you have to implement the feedback and the process discussed. If nothing happens after the conversation, then there is a failure in communication.

It's essential to understand your audience and actively demonstrate that understanding. By employing these components, you can establish a genuine connection with others and show them you value their perspectives, struggles, and desires. This not only increases audience trust but also makes your message more compelling and memorable. In doing so, you lay the foundation for a successful and lasting relationship – one that transcends mere transactional exchanges and paves the way for meaningful and fulfilling interactions.

Communication is an ever-developing skill, something leaders must continuously refine through practice and by taking the time to listen and comprehend what others have to say. One of the common struggles I see with communication is allowing others to speak during conversations. This can be difficult for a lot of individuals who are arrogant, come off as stubborn, or are easily distracted because they are passionate about what they are saying. Many leaders fear their message will be criticized by the person they are speaking with, so they don't make room for the other person to speak. This type of behavior discourages open communication. You need to give the other person an honest opportunity to say what is on their mind and build upon it, whether it's right or wrong or you agree or disagree. If you struggle to leave space for other people to talk, I encourage you to pause more often during conversations to make room for the other person to speak up.

Creating an atmosphere of open communication in my organizations was always a top priority. It was my goal to make each employee feel comfortable and safe to speak up, so I adopted a hands-on philosophy of management. I made it a point to walk around and engage team members directly with point-blank questions. Employees knew I genuinely cared about their tasks and initiatives, which allowed for honest dialogue and the free exchange of ideas. Through this approach, I was able to foster healthy relationships throughout the workplace while making sure everyone felt heard and appreciated. I found myself using the input from my employees to solve problems they may not have otherwise communicated. Seeing the smiles on their faces when I told them they noticed something I hadn't and that we were going to pull together the necessary resources to tackle the problem was incredibly rewarding.

Communicating with employees was a key factor in uncovering some of our biggest issues at my company. By getting out and speaking to the team, I was able to detect problems much earlier. Spending time having candid conversations opened up an avenue for transparent communications, which ultimately prevented potential disasters before they could even happen. Open communication between all facets of the organization was absolutely essential for our success. Whether it was employees, customers, or systems, we had a thorough understanding of the issues facing us, which allowed us to come up with an effective strategy, attacking every element at once rather than piece by piece. This gave us the basis to make more informed decisions and develop plans focused on providing satisfactory solutions for everyone involved.

In this way, open communication acts as a building block for a successful business. Learning how to communicate effectively is key to creating trust within an organization, strengthening relationships, making important connections, and gathering information from different perspectives. With improved communication skills, leaders can continue inspiring change and growth within any organization they are leading.

Preparedness

When you're communicating with your team, whether it's through a presentation, a meeting, or a one-on-one conversation, it is not just the content and structure of what you say that is important but how you deliver it. Many leaders who are unprepared tend to lack confidence in their delivery and fail to successfully communicate their points. They often spend more time straying from the message than elaborating on it. Instead, take the time and effort to ensure your message is clear, concise, and well-structured. When giving a presentation, engaging visuals can back up each point. Investing this time in the presentation of your message will guarantee you finish feeling confident your audience fully understands the message you delivered. You might consider making PowerPoint and having other materials or resources available after a presentation.

Being prepared requires you to know what you plan to deliver before you begin speaking to another person. This is something many managers struggle with because they think they can just wing it. When they do, they end up going on a tangent about a topic they didn't plan on speaking about and may not even cover the topics they intended to cover. Take the time to think through what you want to say and make sure your ideas are logically ordered. It might be beneficial to practice beforehand so you can get comfortable and test out how it sounds when spoken aloud. It doesn't hurt to run something by a coworker or close friend, but if they offer feedback, make sure you understand who and where that feedback is coming from. Having a good handle on the material will also ensure you are better equipped to respond if any questions or issues arise during your meeting or presentation.

In any conversation, I prefer not to rely on a pre-written script or index cards. Instead, I prepare by spending time mastering the content before addressing my audience so I can speak confidently and eloquently. There are many tools available to help you prepare for one-on-one conversations, big meetings, or even keynote addresses. While teleprompters are often helpful for speaking in front of a larger audience, they can also appear distracting if the speaker relies too heavily on them. Knowing the material inside and out allows the presenter to engage far more effectively with their audience and truly deliver impactful commentary.

Many of these tools can be used during presentations or conversations, but I always encourage leaders to use them as a preparation strategy or a backup tool. It can be difficult to remember every nuance of your subject when delivering a lengthy presentation, so it doesn't hurt to keep notes handy. This could be a one-page sheet of information or several index cards with each element and a few essential bullet points. These vital chunks of information are helpful to keep you concise and organized, so you don't miss a major element in your delivery.

Another critical aspect of being prepared is expecting unforeseen challenges or opportunities that may arise in the moment. This preparation enables effective decision-making, maintains a sense of control amidst uncertainty, and demonstrates a strong understanding of factors influencing the outcome. Embracing an inclusive and collaborative approach, a well-prepared leader seeks input from various sources, anticipates potential risks, and encourages a culture of adaptability within their team. By fostering this proactive mentality, leaders can adapt their strategies to navigate the ever-changing dynamics of their environment, ultimately leading their team to thrive and succeed in the face of adversity.

Being prepared can be very beneficial, especially when it comes to accomplishing one's goals. Some may write notes on a piece of paper with what needs to be done and then use a combination of memory techniques and mind mapping to keep themselves organized. Everyone has their unique process for being prepared, so it's important to do what works best for you, and if it does not work for you…modify.

Mannerisms

Mannerisms and body language play an incredibly significant role in the successful communication of leaders. The way a leader carries themselves, their gestures, and their posture can convey confidence, establish authority, and encourage trust in their team. It is not just about what a leader says, but also how they say it. Tone of voice and facial expressions can greatly impact the way a message is received. By mastering the art of non-verbal communication, leaders can foster a sense of unity and direction within their teams, which ultimately allows them to achieve their goals more efficiently. Being mindful of these subtle cues helps leaders build meaningful connections and create a harmonious work environment.

Some of the important mannerisms to be aware of are:

- Posture
- Movement
- Facial expressions and eye contact
- Hand gestures
- Tone
- Dress

Maintaining a strong and steady posture can be invaluable in setting a tone of confidence and professionalism when speaking to an audience of any size. Standing straight with your shoulders back and both feet planted firmly on the ground, not leaning forward or backward is generally a stance of confidence. I highly recommend moving around to engage the audience and keep things interesting. This can involve walking away from the podium or the front of the room. While you should never simply stand behind a podium, it can be a great tool to establish a confident posture. If your goal is to engage your audience, move around the room or stage to make your point and focus on addressing the group as a whole. Walking around can make the audience feel more at ease and able to listen more to what is happening. However, walking around frantically as if you are pacing can be distracting or make the audience feel uneasy.

Even if you're not standing in front of an audience, you still need to maintain a confident posture. If you are leaning forward in your chair and notice the other person leaning back, there's a good chance they are feeling attacked by your posture. If you are leaning very far back in your chair, it shows the other person you don't care about the topic you are speaking about, so it's important to find the middle ground of sitting up straight and leaning ever-so-slightly forward to show you are engaged and listening.

It is also important to be mindful of your facial expressions throughout—an occasional smile or nod conveys friendliness and making confident eye contact serves as an extra layer of connection with the audience. In a more intimate conversation, people become more attuned to these seemingly small details. If an employee is sharing serious or critical information with you, it's important not to laugh or grin from ear to ear because they could interpret that as you not taking them seriously.

Eye contact is something we often take for granted until we notice a lack of it. If we are talking to someone who is constantly looking away, at the ground, or rolling their eyes, we immediately assume they are uninterested in a conversation. It shows they have checked out. Maintaining eye contact with a soft gaze shows interest, engagement, and empathy.

Your hand gestures can communicate a lot as well. In psychology, there is a practice related to interactive behaviors, which are the things you do to make people feel comfortable in a table setting. This includes placing a hand on the desk, not tapping your fingers, and putting your hands together or moving them to the right or left to make certain points. They can be used as a sign of welcome or to emphasize key points. A fist on the table or podium can also be used to emphasize a point, but some may also interpret it as aggression so it's important to be aware of your tone and your audience when using hand gestures. If someone is wringing their hands together or has their arms crossed in front of their chest it can mean they are either angry or nervous.

By doing this, you can use certain mannerisms and hand gestures to stress key points in your message. This helps me bring people into discussions and emphasize topics effectively. All of this movement is useful when creating an interactive environment with listeners, but it's important not to distract them by moving around too much or fidgeting. Finding the right balance between movement and focus can truly engage an audience.

When it comes to tone, consider the volume of your voice. If you are delivering a presentation to a large group, you will need to make sure everyone can hear you. Do a mic check beforehand and again when you begin speaking to confirm everyone can clearly hear you. It's very unlikely you would need to project your voice in a one-on-one conversation; however, it is important to speak firmly about what needs to be conveyed. Nobody likes a directive, so be polite when offering suggestions to others.

The tone you set when dealing with an employee can have a major outcome on how they process what you are saying and how they choose to take action moving forward. The last thing you want is an employee walking out with an attitude that they aren't going to help you. If someone doesn't handle your feedback well, it's unlikely they will implement it, which could negatively impact the organization.

How you dress also says a lot about how you present yourself. If the valedictorian speaker at a college commencement ceremony was wearing anything other than their gown, sashes, and cap, we are likely to question whether or not this is a graduation ceremony. Although we won't always be able to align ourselves with others' expectations, how we dress can play a big role in how others view us in a professional setting. We have all heard the expression "dress for success," but leaders dress in a way that relates to what the environment asks for, rather than what we envision it "should be." If you are a leader in finance, it's likely appropriate for you to wear a suit or at least a sports coat, but it's unlikely you would wear your suit to the company's yearly barbeque. If you are a leader working in a homeless shelter, you probably wouldn't wear a suit unless you were going to a formal gala event. As a leader, it's important to dress for your environment rather than dress for success.

Goal-Oriented

By starting with a clear, concise objective in conversations, you will be better equipped to organize the information you share effectively and foster a sense of purpose among your listeners. A well-defined goal helps to create a productive discourse by reducing the chances of divergent conversations and enabling you to assess your performance and make improvements as necessary. I don't think anyone can be above average if they are not goal-oriented. They can do just enough to get by, but they won't be successful. Implementing this focused approach not only presents you as a knowledgeable and confident speaker but also facilitates deeper comprehension of the subject matter by the audience, ultimately leading to a more significant impact on your message.

It may be tempting to add some extra embellishments or acknowledgments, but these should only be done after the focus has already been established. Before delving into the main points, I like to put my audience into inquiry mode by posing questions and allowing them to probe around to identify any issues or concerns that need to be addressed, then I build from there. Remember, your audience will come from a variety of different backgrounds and experiences, so it's important to assess where they are currently in the understanding of the topic you are presenting. The goal of the presentation should be as clear as possible from the start. This way, everyone can focus their efforts on getting us closer to achieving that goal with meaningful solutions. Once you are done presenting, you should assess again to ensure everyone in your audience understands the message you are trying to convey.

No matter what we are talking about, being goal-oriented helps to keep everyone on the same page and working toward the same end. The goals must be defined by you, as the leader, or else you run the risk of everyone on your team creating their own and causing chaos.

Don't wait until there is a problem in need of solving or a fire to put out. Define your individual and company goals early, track the progress as you go, and decide when changes need to be made based on past performance.

Competencies

A competency is the ability to do something successfully or efficiently. It's a step above a skill or the maturing of a skill because being competent involves having knowledge and skills that enable a person or an organization to take appropriate actions in various situations and to recognize when further knowledge or help is needed to complete a task correctly for optimal results. You may be naturally inclined as a writer, which means you have a skill in writing, but you need to practice that skill and apply it to become competent. Individuals can work on competence by setting attainable goals, assessing their abilities, and being open to learning new ideas to advance their knowledge base. There's no single path to achieving competence, as everyone has their strengths and weaknesses they need to address accordingly. With the proper dedication and drive, anyone can become competent at a particular skill or body of knowledge.

Competence within an organizational structure is integral to a company's overall success and can be broken down into three major elements. These elements work synergistically to ensure the organization operates efficiently and effectively to achieve its objectives. Understanding three key elements of competence—decision-making, people management, and project management—helps us appreciate the importance of each component in the accomplishment of the company's goals.

Decision-making

A successful leader must possess a strong understanding of their field or industry to make well-informed decisions that benefit the company. This begins with accurately identifying issues or opportunities, analyzing potential courses of action, and ultimately determining what direction to take. It is crucial for leaders to possess strong critical thinking and problem-solving abilities to give strategic guidance to their employees. Companies thrive when their management team can evaluate various scenarios and choose the most appropriate course of action to achieve the desired outcomes.

People Management

People management involves a leader's ability to manage their team's ability to carry out tasks skillfully and efficiently. This is not only technical and specialized tasks, but also effective communication and collaboration among team members. Providing employees with proper training and education is critical for them to hone their competencies and contribute meaningfully to the organization. Employees who possess diverse skill sets can adapt to changes in the industry and help their teams overcome obstacles. Additionally, employees who are skilled communicators are better equipped to share ideas, collaborate on projects, and resolve conflicts, further contributing to a company's productivity and growth. A competent people manager will be able to foster a culture of continuous improvement and effectively delegate tasks to employees based on their skills and strengths.

Project Management

Project management plays a vital role in the overall functioning of an organization. To manage a project effectively, a manager must have the ability to monitor progress, provide feedback, and motivate their team. Competent project managers will have an aptitude for recognizing potential roadblocks and navigating challenges that arise throughout the course of a project. In this case, project management requires flexibility and adaptability. Leaders expect challenges and setbacks and view them as an opportunity to learn, grow, and do better next time. When a leader excels in project management, processes run smoother and become more efficient over time because they are always looking for ways to improve.

Competence in an organizational structure is a multifaceted concept. When all three elements work together harmoniously, organizations are better equipped to accomplish their goals and maintain a competitive edge in their respective industries. By fostering an environment that values competence at every level, companies can ensure their long-term success and growth. When any of these competencies are missing or substandard, it can be detrimental to teams and their objectives.

For example, a leader who lacks competence in the area of people management might rush their employees to complete a task quickly instead of taking the prudent amount of time, which can often lead to adverse effects such as unnecessary stress and anxiety that undermine their confidence and ability to perform well. In most cases, such an approach can negatively affect the quality of the task, which is a reflection of the company. This is why successful leaders will always take a collaborative approach to complete tasks.

While emphasizing urgency is crucial in some instances, managers should avoid creating a constant state of emergency for their employees. When we operate from a fire-drill mentality, we put our employees on edge and in a constant state of fight-or-flight mode. Eventually, this mentality wears on them and can make it difficult for them to sustain successful employment over time. Rather than focusing on all the negatives, potential challenges, or setbacks that have already occurred, managers should recognize and celebrate accomplishments and provide constructive feedback to encourage continued growth. By acknowledging their employee's hard work and effort, managers can motivate their employees to maintain high-quality standards consistently. This approach gives employees a sense of fulfillment, encouraging them to take pride in their work and take ownership of their roles. Leaders should find the right balance between urgency and fostering a positive work culture, motivating employees to maintain high-quality standards consistently.

Trust

As a leader, it is important to remember your team members are capable professionals with valuable skills and insights. By demonstrating trust in their abilities, you will build the confidence needed for everyone to work together in harmony and create successful outcomes. Involving your team members in planning to create effective strategies using their experience and knowledge empowers them and boosts morale. Regular constructive feedback is another way to build trust and help employees develop their skills while showing recognition for the hard work they have put in. An environment of mutual respect flourishes with trust between the leaders and their teams, setting them up to reach new heights of success.

As a higher-level manager, recognizing the efforts and challenges of those directly responsible for managing employees is essential. Providing support to these managers, making yourself available for communication with on-the-ground personnel, and being aware of their needs and ideas surrounding process improvements or product development should be a top priority. By effectively supporting the work being done, both at an individual and organizational level, higher-level managers can help to create an environment of trust that prioritizes both professional growth and company success.

As a leader, you must have confidence and trust in your team to move the project forward. One way of doing this is by providing them with the right level of meaningful support and resources necessary to be successful in their work. This helps make employees feel appreciated and motivated to do their best. Communicating the "why" of an important project or task will also build trust as well as collaboration and teamwork.

If this trust is broken, it can lead to problems of self-worth among the individuals working on the task at hand. For example, if a company knows they are going to merge departments but fails to tell the employees before they hear it through the grapevine, employees can feel like they were treated unjustly or like they aren't doing enough at their job to be taken seriously. If mistakes are made and are not adequately handled, they will begin to think their work is no longer valued or trusted by superiors. It's important to show appreciation and encourage employees, especially when they make mistakes, and discuss how to prevent future errors. This level of transparency builds trust between everyone in the company because no one is blaming each other, and everyone is looking to succeed in a shared goal.

Negotiation

Leaders should be able to facilitate productive conversations through negotiation to reach a mutual agreement everyone is happy with. This will help build trust between colleagues, enabling them to work together more effectively in the future. By focusing on outcomes rather than arguments, it is easier to find common ground, which reduces conflict overall and helps speed up decision-making processes.

Successful negotiation also leads to better deals for the organization from business-to-business (B2B) and business-to-customer (B2C) sales activities. By understanding how the other party operates and their interests, leaders can craft an offer that benefits both parties involved in the transaction. Negotiations can secure better terms for the company and open up new opportunities that would not have been possible without these discussions taking place. Effective negotiating skills enable leaders to save time and money when working on projects. Through clearly outlining expectations at the beginning of negotiations, it is less likely either party will waste time or resources on something that could have been avoided by openly discussing details beforehand.

A leader needs to be in a position where they can effectively monitor and assign tasks, identify potential roadblocks, and be open to creative solutions and new ideas from team members. If an employee is struggling to complete a task, negotiating with them to adjust their schedule or work hours to maximize productivity may be an effective solution. This process involves working with employees to find a mutually beneficial solution for both the employee and the organization. If the manager believes the employee is a keeper and is simply struggling, the manager needs to be flexible and willing to make necessary adjustments to ensure employees are supported and tasks are accomplished effectively. However, if the employee is unqualified or not the right fit, then may be necessary to manage them out of the organization.

This can be one of the hardest decisions to make in management and leadership. In any size company, you are going to have departmental managers who aren't going to want to fire someone without first running it by the leader in charge or the HR department because of fear of a lawsuit. With this in mind, the leadership team needs to work together with the manager to decide if this employee is someone worth coaching into an effective contributor to the organization or if they are better off cutting their losses and moving on. I have also been in situations where we discussed firing someone who turned out to be one of our best employees six months down the line.

Interestingly enough, I had a manager once who was struggling and constantly getting frustrated with his job because we didn't have the right operations staff for him to get his job done effectively. He eventually found another job, and it turned out to be a good move for him because he received the support he needed. I learned a lot from that experience because I wasn't being the responsive leader I needed to be. He was certainly capable, but I wasn't there for him in the way he needed at that time. It was a tough loss for me but a positive lesson for the future.

Encouraging employees to come up with new ideas is essential to driving innovation in a company. If a team member has an idea to improve a process but faces certain constraints, involve both the employee and the manager in a discussion to find a solution that works for everyone. This approach makes the employee feel valued and respected, increasing their motivation to work harder and smarter. It also fosters a culture of creativity and innovation while promoting the overall success of the organization.

Well-developed negotiation skills provide numerous advantages for leaders looking to foster stronger relationships, get better deals, and increase productivity within their teams, so managers need to practice these techniques whenever possible to ensure success moving forward.

Sellable

A good leader must be an effective salesperson. Being able to persuade and influence others is key for a leader to get their team on board with ideas and initiatives. Having excellent communication skills and speaking with confidence are both crucial for being effective at selling ideas and getting people to take action. Leaders can demonstrate how their idea or initiative will benefit the organization, as well as show how they align with the company's core values.

One of the biggest challenges in management is selling the importance of every employee's role in the process. All too often, employees may feel like their position isn't as important or impactful when compared to others. As a leader, it is essential to make sure each employee recognizes their role in the process and its importance to the overall success of the company. Creating a culture where every employee feels valued and essential to the success of the company, regardless of their role, will help ensure the best quality end product or service possible. By communicating with employees regularly, managers can ensure each team member recognizes every role is valuable and everyone is working together to achieve greatness in any productive endeavor.

Many workers in an automobile assembly line may not think of their job as being especially important. However, each person must do their part in the company's goal of producing safe and functional vehicles for customers. Just imagine what would happen if one crucial piece went missing from the car's construction, like the wheels or the lug nuts. Without the worker who puts them on, the entire assembly line process would come to a grinding halt. No matter which step of the production line each employee holds responsibility for—from putting in the fuel tank to checking rearview mirror functionality— everyone has an equally important role to play in creating this vehicle. It's up to the leader of these individuals to make sure each employee understands their importance so teamwork can be embraced towards creating quality products.

Every employee in an organization is essential for a company to deliver the highest quality product possible. Their commitment to their job can provide an opportunity for creativity and innovation, which boosts their chances of success. By encouraging employees to take initiative and collaborate with colleagues, managers provide fertile ground for product development and improvement. When a department succeeds in delivering a quality product, they earn recognition from their superiors and get a chance to try something new. Leaders should always strive to foster this kind of environment by motivating their employees with positive reinforcement, so they can keep developing higher-quality products that contribute to the company's overall success.

A leader's job of selling the concept to their employees is one of immense importance and responsibility. They should act as head cheerleaders, creating enthusiasm and delighting employees whenever and wherever possible, which further drives customer satisfaction and loyalty to the company. The efforts made through sellability will, over time, yield tangible results for the company itself.

Openness

In the modern workplace, knowledge sharing is essential to success and growth. By sharing information across departments and teams, organizations can benefit from better collaboration, improved productivity, and increased innovation. Knowledge sharing allows for greater connection between team members and departments, as everyone has access to the same information. This improves communication between team members and enables them to collaborate more effectively on projects. When different employees share their expertise with each other, it encourages an open dialogue, which can lead to new ideas and innovative solutions that wouldn't have been possible without such collaboration.

By encouraging employees to share their knowledge with others, there is a greater sense of ownership over any given project or task within the organization. When employees feel supported in contributing their knowledge, it increases job satisfaction and leads to higher levels of engagement with the company's objectives. When it comes time for employee development or training initiatives, a culture of knowledge sharing allows for cost-effective learning opportunities as mentors can be easily identified both internally and externally. Creating an environment where knowledge exchange is encouraged amongst colleagues brings many valuable benefits both on an organizational level as well as for individual employees pursuing personal development goals. It is crucial that managers take the initiative in promoting a culture of open communication where all team members feel comfortable sharing their expertise.

Knowledge sharing does not just apply to employees though. Leaders who can connect their personal experiences with current management practices will portray confidence, wisdom, and a true understanding of success. In management, the person at the top may not always be aware of what's happening beneath them. They often become so involved in their work that the exchange of knowledge and information between them and other employees becomes minimal. Effective leaders don't just possess the knowledge and experience necessary to lead; they also have the capacity to share this information with others.

With valuable skills, strategies, and lessons learned in their back pocket, those at the top can create an atmosphere of trust and transparency for their team by providing clear guidance and direction. On a practical level, having access to resources such as databases or libraries of documents helps streamline processes and reduce errors due to incorrect information being passed down multiple levels at once.

THOUGHT MANAGEMENT

- How can leaders effectively communicate with their teams and stakeholders, considering different communication styles and preferences?

- What strategies can leaders employ to improve their preparedness for important conversations, meetings, and presentations?

- How can leaders use their mannerisms and body language to build trust and create a positive and inclusive work environment?

- Why is competence important for leaders in decision-making, people management, and project management, and how can leaders foster a culture of continuous learning and growth within their teams to enhance overall competence?

CHAPTER 3

CLIMB THE MOUNTAIN

"A genuine leader is not a searcher for consensus, but a molder of consensus."

MARTIN LUTHER KING, JR.

Not many start at the top in life or business. Most of us must put in the hard work to get where we are looking to go or we will stay stuck. Those who are given an advantage in life might get to the top without having to work for it, but the truth is, they usually don't stay at the top for too long because when something comes easy, we take it for granted. Regardless of where you are starting from, there is no reason you cannot be successful. Throughout my career, I have always looked at the mountain for what is at the top, not the winding road or obstacles standing in the way, and that's the mindset all great leaders need to have.

Hierarchy

Just like in societies, hierarchies have existed in organizations in some form for as long as anyone can remember, even if it was a basic or even unspoken chain of command. In a most basic sense, these hierarchies tell you who is the leader and who should be the follower. Founders are responsible for creating a system of hierarchy in their companies. Though companies may evolve and change ownership over the years, the established hierarchy usually remains the same.

Since hierarchy is such an integral aspect of business, there should be an executive team member or an administration responsible for reviewing and fine-tuning it regularly to promote efficiency in management, systems, processes, and anything that happens within the organization. However, in most cases, this simply does not exist. When we think of an organization that has a CEO or COO, their word is what it is, and everything else is the highway. In other words, they have the final say no matter what. But to truly be successful in any function of your organization, you have to embrace the crucial success factors of the department, which can be achieved through effective communication at all levels and between those levels.

Without efficient communication, you cannot have an effective hierarchy. Within the hierarchy, vertical and horizontal communication should be defined. The channels for passing information from the top to the bottom and vice-versa should be distinct, so individuals at the bottom automatically know how to communicate with those at the top, identifying who needs to hear what and when.

A company's organizational chart is a clear representation of its hierarchy, and it is useful for both internal and external stakeholders. At the top, we have the CEO or the president. Below are usually members of the executive team or C-suite such as the COO, CFO, or CHRO. Based on the C-suite roles, this is where the chart breaks down into divisions based on operations, quality control, compliance, accounting, and human resources, to mention a few. For a successful establishment of the hierarchy, all of these departments have to coexist and work effectively. Even though the CHRO may not directly oversee employees in the finance division, they are still responsible for ensuring those employees receive performance reviews, have a space for filing complaints, and are treated in compliance with labor laws.

Most organizations do not have a simple top-down hierarchy. In fact, successful companies look at all those pieces and understand how they relate to each other. This is one of the hardest yet most important undertakings. If this were to be expressed using strings to connect roles based on who reports to whom, then it would include lines drawn across departments and in between different parts of the hierarchy, capturing how people interact and intersect with each other.

Build It or Inherit It

Founders are often tasked with building hierarchies, while new business leaders are likely to inherit one. However, that's not to say you can't buy an existing company and do a complete overhaul of the hierarchy, which is arguably even more challenging than starting from scratch. Building a hierarchy from scratch is not an easy task, but it can be done in three steps:

1. Define: Leaders clearly define the organization's hierarchy, outlining who is responsible for what and how information moves up the ladder.

2. Interchange: This is where you begin drawing the lines vertically, horizontally, or even diagonally to show the successful flow of communication. In general, this is how we understand the relationships within the hierarchy.

3. Evaluate: Just like any other goal or system in your organization, it is mandatory to evaluate the hierarchy. How does it work? How effective is it? What can be improved? Should we change the procedures? These are all questions that need to be asked during the evaluation phase.

To some extent, building a hierarchy can be a recruitment nightmare because you, or someone else in your organization, will have to recruit the right kind of individual for the right job to ensure there is effective communication between all the involved departments. The recruitment process can make or break the hierarchy, so it's important to recruit individuals who generically understand the kind of process you are dealing with and have familiarity with the inner workings of your industry. This can be applied both in small and big companies. Even if a new recruit tells you they can handle what you are hiring them to do, you need to assess their current skill level and prior work experience.

Amazon's success cannot be attributed to its pre-existing functionality; instead, it was because they sought out those who could think outside the box and focus on the elements of customer service they were looking to achieve. During Amazon's initial stages of creating their delivery system, people questioned what they were doing because they were not using traditional delivery service carriers such as UPS or FedEx. What most people did not recognize is that Amazon spent an adequate amount of time working on the hierarchy and developing successful hubs in specific areas to expedite delivery.

Amazon also did not hire people for the sake of hiring or go out looking for employees who have worked for other famous companies. Instead, they trained their people from scratch and evaluated the outcome by identifying the positives and the negatives of the delivery structure utilized by FedEx and UPS. They utilized customer input and polished their system based on the information they received. When customers said they wanted their orders delivered the next morning, Amazon made it happen. For customers who didn't want their packages to sit outside if they were delivered when they weren't home, Amazon set up hubs where people could pick them up.

While it may seem like Amazon was able to successfully implement these changes overnight, they did come up with several ideas that did not work out. One of their ideas was to drop off packages using drones, but that has not, as of yet, come to fruition – although it still may in the future! Taking your time to build such an organization does not guarantee success. It could be a tough undertaking or a smooth one, but in either case, it all boils down to how well the organization works to achieve this.

When you're inheriting an organization, the steps are different because you need to carry out an evaluation of the current organizational structure upfront using feedback from current leaders, employees, customers, and even competitors, as well as keeping track of any challenges or successes you see within the current structure. The steps for inheriting an organizational structure are:

1. Evaluate

2. Identify and define solutions

3. Retain buy-in

4. Reevaluate

Performing an evaluation allows you to identify how the entity you are taking over is performing. This makes the work easier for you by providing information on what ought to be restructured, the wins and losses, and consequently, what needs to be done to move forward. After the evaluation, you will identify solutions for the areas of improvement and define the changes that should be implemented.

Because you are entering a new environment with people who are used to conducting things in a certain way using a certain structure for a given period of time, you will need to retain their buy-in. To implement any changes in an organization, you need people to have your back. It will take time to build trust with them so it's important to be patient so they can trust in the changes you intend to implement. Effective communication should be used here to your advantage to explain the changes that need to be implemented and why they need to be made.

It is important to integrate the employees into the process as well because they play a vital role as the first people who interact with your customers. They know how the customer feels about the products or services being provided, if the services provided or products delivered are in line with the goals and objectives of the organization, and if the customers' needs were served. If the customers' needs are met, that builds the reputation of the business and helps it grow. These are things the employees usually have firsthand information about, making them important players in facilitating the success of the organization.

Whether starting from scratch or inheriting an organization, the goal is to get to the same place in the end. The path will be different and have different elements, but both approaches deal with the same essential aspects, and evaluation is key to both.

I was once told about a company in Connecticut that built ships in a bottle. They have been doing this for over 150 years and continue to create quality ships. In fact, they created the "best" quality ships in a bottle. Tourists loved them even though they were very expensive, and collectors continued purchasing them throughout the company's existence due to their high quality and rareness. When they were asked what they attributed their success to, they claimed that they never changed anything. But to be in business for that long and not change anything is entirely unlikely, especially since the people who made these ships 150 years ago are not the same people who made them 100 years or even 50 years ago.

In a later article, the company was asked how they managed to build the best quality ships for that long, and the grandson of the gentleman who founded the company said it was made possible by planning and execution but most importantly by employees. According to him, you can hire many employees to do a lot of things, but the employees who make their ships are specialists. They are required to go through a year of internship before being allowed to produce an end product to be sold to a traditional customer like a tourist. When it comes to ships purchased by collectors, the employees must go through another year of apprenticeship and another year of making ships for traditional customers before being assigned to make custom models for collectors. This company offered employees an opportunity to learn a skill that was almost extinct but gave them a livelihood. It also allowed employees to be the best at what they do and continue giving to the customers on the outside despite the declining market.

As I read the article, I asked myself how they could ensure their business was going to grow. Then, I realized that with the rate at which things are changing due to new technology, mass production, and machines carrying out most tasks, individuals appreciate having something unique that was made by hand. They value it more and are willing to pay more for it. The article emphasized employee management and how the employees bought into the hierarchy of the organization, which attributes to their success. No matter if you're a founder or the leader of a pre-existing business, you have to ensure you build a hierarchy that fosters, mentors, and trains the employees you hire to be the best of the best no matter what industry you are in.

A lot of employees start a company or have an existing company, and they like to say they are family. In this case, they are not family by blood, but they are working in a family-like environment fueled by cooperation and mentorship. This type of environment allows for constructive criticism and a metaphorical slap on the wrist when necessary.

Then, there are companies that are literally family-owned. During my coaching and consulting years, I found this type of environment to be troublesome for two main reasons. First, there tends to be a great deal of resentment inside these companies between different family members. Second, nepotism is rampant in this environment, and promotions are given to family members because they are considered next in line. Whether or not they want the job or have the experience to be in the position, they accept it because of the money.

In some cases, the owner's child knows they are going to be the one to take over, so they work hard and prepare to do a good job when they take over. In other situations, the opposite is true. Rather than their child working hard to earn their spot, it is simply handed to them as a result of nepotism. They are given opportunities other people in the company do not get simply because they are family. This type of culture can destroy a company, especially if the person taking over does not understand the management of the company.

A beer distribution company in Alabama has turned out to be the largest distributor in the state. Their hierarchy was started by the parents, and when they died, their son took over. The son did everything in his power to make sure the legacy lived on. He learned the ways of the company and came up through the ranks. He bought new technology, implemented new delivery and management protocols, and made the company even better than how the parents left it. He earned his spot as the company's president. He then had sons and taught them about the business, and they started running their branches. Unfortunately, the sons did not have children of their own, so they wouldn't be able to pass the business down to another generation. At this point, they agreed to sell the company to a buyer with a contract stipulating the father could still work there.

Unfortunately, the greatest lie told by potential buyers of companies is, "We like what you are doing here, you make tons of money, and for that reason, we are not going to change anything." I've heard this lie many times, and the beer distributor heard it too. After purchasing the company, the buyers' egos got to them in just nanoseconds, and they began dismantling the traditions that had been successful for years because they thought the company was not performing as successfully as it could be. In many cases, the buyers who end up purchasing these companies do not have an understanding of how the business runs. Instead of taking time to understand the hierarchies in place, they take less than a minute to destroy everything good about it.

When Elon Musk purchased Twitter, he reduced the staff members from tens of thousands of employees down to a thousand, levelling the hierarchy in place. With such a massive reduction in staff, it makes me wonder how they could be as successful as Twitter had been before. However, it's quite possible Musk let go of the employees who did not see his vision or those whom he simply couldn't justify their position in the new hierarchy he was creating. At the time of writing this, the future of Twitter is still uncertain, and I am sitting back waiting to see the end result because it could be one of the biggest business transformations I see in my lifetime.

Rewards, Motivation, and Recognition

Within the hierarchy, the higher-ups are responsible for informing those who work under them when they have done a good job and when they need to make improvements. When a good job has not been done, they need to communicate this constructively by informing them what they need to improve on and how to ultimately support them in getting to the next level. The next level could be qualifying for a bonus, receiving recognition, or any other motivation that will have them working extra hard.

Some employees make massive differences within a company in one way or another. They may improvise in a way that saves the company a great deal of money or they may come up with ideas to improve a product or service. These employees deserve some type of special recognition beyond salaries and bonuses. While monetary rewards can go a long way in motivating employees, recognition is another way of rewarding them for a job well done. When employees feel their effort at work is being recognized, it increases their motivation to perform better and their likelihood to accept feedback and guidance. When there are areas of improvement, recognizing those improvements a month or three months later creates a positive environment for growth and development.

During my management era, I used recognition as a form of reward, and it proved to be quite effective. I hosted monthly meetings where I called everybody together and handed out awards for perfect attendance or exceeding target goals, as well as recognizing those who supported our charitable activities as volunteers, and employees who worked on a team project and got it done before the stipulated time. I also had a program where such team members were recognized in various ways including certificates, special parking spots in front of the building, or even a voucher to be used to pay for a night out with their significant other.

Another way to reward employees is through opportunities where they can sharpen their skills in socialization and team building. You can do this by hosting events for your employees, where they can socialize without the pressure of work, such as company retreats and other out-of-work activities. We liked to encourage our teams to partake in activities that helped the community at large. We developed a program where every team member could take two days off per month to engage in charitable work at a shelter or a food pantry nearby. While not everyone took part in this, we always had recognition for those who spent their time making a positive impact in our community. Rewarding your employees helps contribute to their ability to climb the mountain in the workplace because it gives them the motivation to do better. As they keep doing good things, they are going to be the top performers and the leaders of tomorrow.

Motivation can be ambiguous to some degree. Some individuals simply cannot be motivated because they don't have the desire within, but there are also those who you have to encourage to slow down because they are constantly working too hard and pushing themselves beyond their limits. There are so many ways to motivate your team. You could recognize what they need and give them the tools or resources to be successful in their goals, you could work with them on a task to show you recognize their efforts, or you could provide them with an opportunity to develop their skills further.

If one of your managers resigns before you can fill their position, you might offer an employee the opportunity to fill that position in the interim by saying something like, "Jane, we have a position we would like you to take on. I do not think you are ready for it right now, but we want to give you the opportunity to understand it more as you build your confidence and gather experience. We need you to keep doing the good job we know you have been doing while keeping this position afloat. This will help you gain experience to tackle other jobs within the company when positions open up." Telling them that will motivate them, while also allowing you the time you need to hire a qualified person for the job.

However, we should never force someone to do something not in their current job description if they don't want to. All we can do is offer them the opportunity and see if they take us up on it. If they choose to move forward, we can then recognize them for their undertaking and going above and beyond what was required of them.

When leaders motivate, understand, and care about what their employees are accomplishing, they can help them climb the mountain by recognizing and rewarding them in front of other leaders. By endorsing other employees, you help increase employee retention and morale. This may seem ambitious, but this is what employee development is about when you are a leader.

THOUGHT MANAGEMENT

- How can leaders establish and maintain an effective hierarchy within their organizations to promote efficient management, communication, and collaboration among different departments?

- What are the challenges and strategies involved in building a hierarchy from scratch, and how does it differ from inheriting an existing organizational structure?

- How can leaders effectively reward, motivate, and recognize their employees to boost their performance and create a positive work environment?

- What lessons can be learned from successful companies like Amazon and the ship-building company to emphasize the importance of nurturing and developing the skills and talents of employees to achieve long-term success

CHAPTER 4

MANAGEMENT 999

"Do you want to know who you are? Don't ask.
Act! Action will define you…"

THOMAS JEFFERSON

For those of you familiar with college courses, you have likely seen Introduction to Business 100, Working Skillfully in Marketing 210, or Operations & Supply Chain Management 340. The number for the course is an indicator of the level of intensity for learning. While most 100-level classes are introductory courses to a topic with general overviews, the higher the course level, the more complex and specific the information gets. Because management is an all-encompassing, inclusive process from everything from A-Z, I call this section Management 999. This includes all the courses you may have taken, the practices you learned from experience, the people you interact with, and the feedback you give and receive. Effective management involves leaders at all levels coming together to create a successful organization.

There must be a solid process in management for it to be effectively led. The process has to give effective feedback to leaders, so they know where they are at all times. If you look at building out this process, you have to have the worker bees on the front lines doing the work, the managers managing the pipelines and process, and the leaders have to have the vision and overall understanding to make changes. Effective management can help the whole hierarchy function at a better pace and a higher level of efficiency.

Lead; Don't Manage

Effective leadership is centered around creating an environment that enables individuals to thrive, allowing them the autonomy to carry out their assigned tasks without the fear of making costly mistakes. The role of a leader is to support their team, be there to lend a helping hand in times of need, and provide guidance and assistance that steers their team in the right direction. This approach empowers individuals to take ownership of their tasks while their superiors provide support and guidance when necessary. Ultimately, a leader's primary goal is to encourage their team to perform at their best and continually nourish their skill sets to achieve excellence. Assessing and providing constructive feedback on their team's performance is an integral aspect of effective leadership. By doing so, leaders can identify areas where team members could improve, rectify issues, and facilitate their personal and professional growth.

On the other hand, the role of a manager involves overseeing the workflow of a team, ensuring all tasks are completed promptly.

Although an individual can possess both leadership and managerial qualities, these two roles operate in distinct functional areas. Leadership primarily focuses on providing direction and motivation, attaining goals, and fostering personal growth in subordinates. It involves passing down years of accumulated knowledge to help others progress in their careers and eventually assume leadership positions themselves. It is crucial to maintain separation between management and leadership, as their respective roles differ significantly.

Micromanagement is a clear example that distinguishes leadership from management. When managers micromanage, they stifle employee recognition and establish a culture of negativity. A good leader acknowledges the detrimental effects of micromanagement and fosters an environment where employees can take initiative and make decisions independently. They provide support and guidance to their team when needed but ultimately trust their employees' capabilities and empower them with the autonomy to execute tasks. In turn, this not only boosts productivity and morale but also highlights the leader's exceptional skills in cultivating a positive and high-performing team.

A great example of effective leadership is exemplified by a highly skilled doctor who, to care for his ailing wife, decided to reduce his weekly work schedule. Recognizing the utmost importance of ensuring the continuity of high-quality healthcare for his patients, he appointed a female physician's assistant (PA) to take charge of his work responsibilities. The PA possessed an impressive level of proficiency and experience, so she was entrusted with the responsibility of delivering the same level of care and patient management as her predecessor. The doctor gave his team the autonomy to take charge of patient care and decision-making while maintaining the presence and availability to provide professional guidance and advice as deemed necessary. The PA was granted the authority to lead and make decisions on behalf of the physician while seeking professional counsel from him when the need arose.

This approach to leadership, which is characterized by delegation, guidance, trust, and mutual respect, provides an excellent example of how an effective leader can successfully navigate challenging situations and empower their team toward delivering desired outcomes. Such exemplary leadership qualities foster trust and confidence in the team's abilities while enhancing the quality of care delivered to patients, which is a crucial aspect of any healthcare institution. Generally, in the medical profession, there is a common tendency among doctors to simply instruct their team on what to do without providing any meaningful explanation or engagement, but exceptional leaders understand the importance of taking the time to explain their thought processes and ensure their team is executing tasks properly. This approach fosters a more productive team dynamic.

When leaders provide their team with explanations and engage them in the decision-making process, team members can better understand the reasoning behind their tasks. By taking the time to explain their thought processes, leaders can avoid costly mistakes and ensure their team is executing tasks in the most efficient and effective manner possible. This leads to a more productive team, a greater sense of fulfillment for team members, and a higher level of commitment and investment in the company as they can see the impact of their work.

This ultimately results in a higher-quality output and a positive image for the company.

Effective leadership hinges on cultivating the right kind of leadership style and promoting strong collaborative relationships with team members. Micromanaging, which can inadvertently result in creating mini versions of oneself, runs counter to this goal. By modeling desired behaviors and practices, people are more likely to replicate a leader's example, so it is imperative for leaders to have faith in the capabilities of their team members and trust them to carry out their job responsibilities effectively.

In a truly collaborative workplace culture, supporting team members' self-actualization and trusting in their abilities is paramount. By acknowledging the education and skill sets of team members and empowering them to utilize those skills, leaders create an environment for increased initiative, creativity, and productivity. However, it's important to still monitor your team and provide feedback. Constructive criticism can still be offered in a non-micromanaging manner. By providing feedback on specific actions and behaviors rather than attempting to scrutinize every task, leaders can help team members improve their skills and performance. It is also essential for leaders to remember they are part of a team, not at the top of a hierarchy. By modeling collaboration and a supportive attitude, leaders can empower team members to work together towards shared goals and common objectives.

Efficient management entails more than just delegating tasks that align with the leader's vision; it also includes routine monitoring of developments carefully. As a result, leaders must engender a positive work environment by establishing constructive relationships with their colleagues and encouraging them to be proactive in their duties. Such an atmosphere facilitates teamwork, which fosters the free flow of ideas, creates an environment conducive to innovation, and increases the chances of achieving business objectives.

Act

In a leadership role, it is imperative to respond quickly when a problem arises within a department or workflow. It is not sufficient to solely manage the issue—you must take action. This includes situations where managers or subordinate leaders within your team encounter such an issue. As the leader, it is your responsibility to take ownership of the problem and address it in a timely manner. Acting on the issue doesn't require you to have all the answers. Rather, it is necessary to identify the problem and engage your team in a discussion to solicit their input on how best to handle it. The issue may be a result of another department not furnishing the necessary resources or a manager being hesitant to address interdepartmental relationships.

To effectively resolve problems within a leadership role, it is imperative to first comprehend the underlying issue fully at hand. Failure to take action will prevent progress and hinder positive resolution. As a leader, it is your responsibility to either take direct action or guide management toward a solution. Acting swiftly and decisively is a critical component of effective leadership. Establishing a step-by-step process that works well with your daily workflow will ultimately lead to the development of a unique plan suited to your team's specific work environment and culture. It is important to recognize that there is no one-size-fits-all approach to problem-solving, as every issue is unique.

By utilizing a more detailed and factual approach to problem-solving, a leader can successfully address any obstacle that may arise. Taking the necessary steps towards fostering a solution-oriented mindset and providing direction to management is crucial to ensuring success within your team's work environment. With the right approach, any challenge can be navigated with clarity and confidence.

The culture of a company can have a profound impact on its success or failure. As leaders, it is our responsibility to establish a nurturing work environment in which employees can find satisfaction in their work, contribute to the achievement of company objectives, and thrive both personally and professionally. To accomplish this, we need to root out damaging practices, such as unproductive criticism, unduly punishing employees for minor errors, and hiring individuals who do not align with the company culture despite their impressive qualifications.

Creating a positive workplace environment can be a difficult undertaking, but it is one of utmost importance. We have all witnessed the stark differences between exceptional and inadequate company cultures, and the latter can result in decreased motivation, heightened employee turnover, and a decrease in overall productivity. By deliberately promoting a supportive culture, we can inspire our employees to be more efficient, effective, and engaged in the work they do.

I have had outstanding experiences with Chick-fil-A due to the well-trained and amicable staff. The employees, from top management to store-level personnel, are highly proficient in their roles and consistently provide top-notch service. One aspect that stands out to me is their response to gratitude, which is a simple, "My pleasure." It's an endearing response that reflects the company's culture of service excellence, which has been cultivated and maintained over many years. This dedication to training and service is the foundation of their success and is the reason their employees' attitudes and performance are consistently of a high standard.

Chick-fil-A has faced criticism from certain individuals due to its founder's unwavering Christian beliefs, which have occasionally resulted in controversial statements and actions. Despite this, I hold a high level of admiration for the company, specifically for its choice to refrain from operating on Sundays. This gesture allows their staff to have quality time with their loved ones, resulting in a commendable display of prioritizing people over profit.

The Chick-fil-A leadership team should be commended for their exceptional ability to instill positive traits in their employees. These traits not only promote efficient communication with customers and colleagues but also facilitate a healthy work-life balance. One can easily observe the impressive teamwork and camaraderie among employees working behind the counter. Rather than having only one employee working on an order, there are typically three or four employees working together to guarantee prompt and efficient service. The level of interdependence among employees is striking to witness as they work in perfect harmony to achieve their common goal.

Because management is a process, you have to build it—and build it with good leaders, managers, and employees who have been trained effectively and want to do the work. Employees need to be trained in culture just as much as they are in their daily tasks and responsibilities. If you can consistently communicate the culture of the company, what you want it to be, and enforce it, your employees will either get behind it to support the company or get out of the way. Have you heard that before?

You can create your culture by developing a standard for your company. Your mission statement will outline the key elements you want in your culture and how you deal with customers. Then, you can establish a process to survey and involve the individuals who work for you at all levels to give their feedback about how everyone can make the culture better for employees and customers. When you ask people questions or ask them what they want, they will tell you, so it's your responsibility to create a process for that communication, interact and listen to what they have to say, and act on that feedback.

If we look at the startups in Silicon Valley, most had free coffee bars, communal spaces for employees to interact, as well as ping pong tables and other games for people to de-stress. All of this became part of the culture of these companies. Companies like Apple, Microsoft, and Google have always prioritized their employees' ability to interact with one another and decompress as needed. Bill Gates once said the greatest value added to their company is when employees talk to one another. He wanted people from different departments to interact with one another because he believed it created an opportunity to solve issues in new ways with unique insights. Because he believed in this, he acted on it and was able to become one of the most successful leaders in the world.

Expert

It is imperative to understand and accept that nobody can truly be an expert on every subject matter. Every one of us has our own distinct strengths and weaknesses. Consequently, some of our actions may be deemed as good, while others may not be viewed as favorable. As a leader, you do not need to be a leading authority in every subject. You simply need to possess an adequate amount of knowledge and expertise relevant to the field you are overseeing. This level of proficiency allows one to inspire confidence in others' abilities as well as cultivate a sense of respect and trust from others.

During a podcast interview, I spoke with a customer relationship manager from Candor Technology, an innovative company offering automation services for the underwriting process in the mortgage lending sector. As we delved into the details of his impressive background, we noted he held not only a bachelor's degree in engineering but also a master's degree in business and a law degree. I couldn't help but comment on his astoundingly diverse skill set. I consider myself to be a person with many varied interests and skills, yet, to date, I have not come across many people who have succeeded in gaining such diverse and extensive knowledge in multiple fields. It's not often someone with an engineering degree has both an MBA and a law degree. His varied educational background rendered him an expert in multiple domains, an aspect his management team highly regarded. His role involved creating novel systems and aiding his team while also ensuring they were in line with legal compliances.

In addition to possessing in-depth knowledge of our fields, we also need to have an understanding of psychology to succeed in our roles. A comprehensive grasp of these two areas will equip us to be successful leaders. When I embarked on my career, I was hired by a Director of Human Resources, who held a degree in philosophy. Because of his degree, he felt like he really understood people in a unique way that no one else could. Initially, he expressed skepticism towards the value of my master's degree in psychology in relation to my job, which was solely based on whatever bias he had toward the study of psychology. However, my experience managing teams of thousands of individuals in my career has taught me a great deal about the significance of understanding their needs, desires, and motivations to enhance their productivity and help them achieve their professional goals.

It became clear to me, and eventually to the Director, that every bit of knowledge and expertise we possess can be leveraged in the workplace, provided we learn how to apply it effectively. However, our formal education alone may not suffice in the business world. We must acquire knowledge and experiences specific to our role to become successful leaders. It takes a combination of general and specialized knowledge to manage a team effectively and propel them toward success.

Medical professionals have numerous resources at their disposal to help them stay informed about the latest products and treatments in the field. Medical pamphlets and articles from medical journals are both common methods doctors use to stay informed about new medications, therapies, and other medical advancements. Staying up to date with these resources is essential because it directly impacts the quality of care that doctors provide for their patients. Consider the case of a doctor who fails to keep up with the latest medical developments. Even if they are an expert in their field, their knowledge would quickly become outdated, and they would be unable to provide the best possible care. Such medical professionals could risk jeopardizing patient safety, as well as their careers, and can be held liable for medical malpractice if they fail to align with contemporary medical standards and practices.

This is why it is particularly important for medical professionals to stay informed about new developments in their field. Attendance at seminars and conferences, networking with peers, and subscribing to reputable medical journals are just some of the ways medical professionals can maintain their expertise. By taking steps to stay informed, they can ensure they are providing the highest quality of care to their patients and upholding their professional responsibilities and values.

In the same way, most professions require a deep knowledge of the latest trends and developments, and leaders are responsible for effectively communicating these to their teams. By doing so, you can ensure everyone is working together towards a common goal, delivering the highest possible service to your clients or customers. By staying up to date on industry developments, you can lead your team with confidence and make informed decisions to achieve organizational success. You can also maintain a competitive edge and build a strong reputation in your field by prioritizing ongoing learning and growth.

To earn the respect of your employees, you need to be able to answer their questions and help them do their job quicker, better, and more efficiently. Being an expert in your field is crucial to becoming a better leader and helping your subordinates advance in their careers.

Many individuals get stuck in a routine and fail to seek out additional development through education or attending seminars, which can limit their growth and development. While employees may learn the best ways to do their jobs over time, receiving constructive criticism and staying informed about industry developments can help them perform even better. As a leader, it's important to encourage your employees at all levels to attend the right seminars and take relevant courses.

It's also incredibly helpful to invite experts to come speak to your team. When I was a college professor, I would invite two or three guest speakers, who were experts in the topics we were studying, to come speak with each of my classes throughout the semester. I found my students appreciated hearing from these experts because they offered unique insights not found in textbooks. They provided advice and guidance on various aspects related to the subject matter, and my students found the experience to be highly beneficial. One thing I have never forgotten is the positive feedback I received from my students regarding the value of these guest speakers. This goes to show the impact one can have by being an expert in an industry, field, or even a specific task at hand.

THOUGHT MANAGEMENT

- How does effective management contribute to the success of an organization, and what are the key components of a solid management process?

- What are the key attributes of effective leadership, and how does it differ from management? Provide examples that illustrate the distinction between leadership and management roles.

- Why is taking prompt action crucial in leadership roles? How can leaders address problems and challenges effectively within their teams or organizations?

- How do expertise and continuous learning impact leadership effectiveness? Provide examples of how being an expert in a field can benefit leaders and their teams, and how leaders can foster a culture of learning and knowledge sharing in their organizations.

CHAPTER 5

MANAGING UP, DOWN, AND LATERAL

"Alone we can do little, together we can do so much."

HELEN KELLER

Management can take all forms—up, down, and lateral. Most staff managers understand what managing down means because you manage the employees who work for you. In recent years, managing up has become more common as employees now feel they are managing those whom they work for, especially when it comes to tasks their managers don't want to do or don't necessarily have the skills to do well. Managing laterally happens when you cross-departmentalize a project or task.

We have to manage those we work for and manage their expectations against what we are delivering. We also must manage those below us to deliver against our expectations and do the work they are required to do to maintain their jobs. On the lateral side, we have to manage all the people who affect how we move along the path of success in our work. This could be vendors who provide resources like shipping services, copy machines, or computer support. You may be depending on another department or another affiliate of the company that affects what you do. It's important to realize there are three different types of management, and you still have to control the process of each of these to be successful while you're dealing with uniquely different people. With all of these different entities, you have to modify your approach to how you manage those people to be successful.

Training

Training is a crucial component of any successful business, and successful leaders prioritize their team's training. While it is possible to hire an individual with prior experience in a similar role, it is rare to find someone who possesses all of the skills and knowledge necessary to perform their new job at the highest level, so it is important to engage in conversations with new hires during the HR screening process to ensure they are a good fit for the job and the company culture.

During candidate interviews, assess their expertise and skills to determine if they have the necessary qualifications for the position and consider their potential for growth and development within the organization. The ability for employees to learn new skills benefits their career progression and maximizes their overall performance in their roles. Businesses are constantly evolving, and so should employee skills and knowledge. The impact of continuous training cannot be overstated, as it provides employees with the tools they need to excel at every aspect of their job, from customer service to technical proficiency. Through training, employees are equipped with the latest techniques and technologies, which allows for the development of new skills and approaches that are critical for the success of any business.

As a leader, there are times when you will come across a potential hire who lacks some of the required skills for the position. It is important to note this is not an unusual occurrence. However, it is crucial to ensure the individual chosen for the role receives the necessary training to perform their duties effectively. It may seem challenging, particularly if the new hire is expected to deliver results immediately, but investing in their training is a wise move that will benefit your organization in the long run. By equipping them with the necessary skills, you are laying a strong foundation for their success within your company and ultimately contributing to achieving your organizational goals.

There are multiple forms of training available, and one can choose the method that suits the job requirement or organizational culture. External courses and books provide a structured approach to learning and are ideal for those who prefer a self-paced environment. However, formal classroom training offers a more interactive experience with hands-on learning opportunities and expert guidance.

On-the-job training is another popular form of training, where new hires are paired with experienced employees who can impart their knowledge and skills to others. This method is especially useful for job roles that require practical expertise, such as in the medical and technical fields. On-the-job training enables new hires to gain hands-on experience and get a clear understanding of their work responsibilities. Not only that, but it also creates mentorship opportunities. It is a great idea to provide this type of on-the-job training to ensure all employees have the skills they need to be successful.

Let's say I own an apartment complex and need to hire a new building manager. After reviewing my checklist, I determined Alice was the best candidate because she met eight out of the ten critical criteria. Despite her impressive qualifications, there were still a couple of areas where she lacked experience. To address this, I would introduce Alice to the department as the new manager, but also provide her with additional guidance in the areas she requires improvement. I might suggest she shadow Judy, who has been with the company for six or seven years and knows how to do those things well. This way, Alice can learn and become proficient in all aspects of the department.

Leadership training is another crucial aspect of improving employee development and success. Great leaders set an example by providing constructive feedback and coaching to their team members as they guide them to achieve their goals. Investing in leadership training programs can aid leaders in developing essential skills like effective communication, problem-solving, and decision-making abilities. As a result, leaders can become more proficient in leading and developing their teams, which will improve employee performance and encourage higher job satisfaction and increased productivity.

Another tangible way to promote ongoing education and training is through offering certification programs within a company. These programs provide employees with the ability to take a range of courses over a set period and earn a certificate upon completion, signifying their expertise in a given area. Providing employees with opportunities for continuing education is crucial. Companies can support their employees' enrollment in a range of institutions, including junior colleges, technical schools, and universities, so employees can hone their abilities and gain new knowledge they can apply to their job responsibilities.

When it comes to more formal training, such as classroom or off-the-shelf training, it's important to customize it to fit the specific needs and culture of the company by using relevant examples and incorporating company values and practices. As a firm believer in customized training, I prefer not to purchase pre-packaged training courses for my team. Instead, I use external courses as a foundation to identify the essential elements that need to be covered, while using prepackaged material for additional input. This approach enables me to tailor the training to the specific needs of my team, resulting in more meaningful and effective learning. I find this personalization approach to be more effective in engaging with my team members than reading off a set of notes from a generic online course. By customizing the training to their specific needs, it's easier to connect with people and ensure they understand the material.

To ensure effective training, it's crucial to have a comprehensive evaluation program in place. At my company, we've found that using a panel of one to three individuals to assess an employee's progress after they've completed the six-week training period yields the best results. During the evaluation, we encourage employees to openly discuss their work and the skills they've acquired during the training period. To determine the effectiveness of our training program in specific areas, we ask employees about particular topics or skills, such as XYZ or ABC. By doing so, we're able to assess whether or not they've been effectively trained in these areas. If an employee demonstrates mastery in these key skill areas, then we know our training program was successful. However, if there are areas in which they are struggling, it's clear we need to make adjustments to improve the program.

Similarly, when establishing a new department and organizing training for a team, it can be beneficial to involve a member of the leadership team in the process. This individual could engage with the trainees and encourage them to evaluate the training program. By doing so, the trainees can provide valuable feedback on what they have learned, areas they would like to further develop, and how the training program will benefit their job performance. By utilizing this feedback, you can refine the training program to better suit the needs of the trainees. This process can also assist with identifying those employees who have a strong desire to learn and improve their job performance, creating a more effective workforce.

When employees have trouble receiving directives from upper management, it is often due to the frustration of receiving instructions from individuals who lack firsthand involvement in the day-to-day operations of the business. Such actions commonly result in a loss of respect for the manager of the entire team. The maintenance of mutual respect between the managerial staff and the team is crucial for the successful accomplishment of business development and workflow management goals.

Developing competent leaders is a vital aspect of any business. Providing training to managers on how to become effective leaders and instilling the essential skills and values in them can significantly enhance the work environment's positivity and productivity. Employees who enjoy their work are more likely to actively pursue opportunities to advance within the company, which can lead to better organizational outcomes such as increased innovation, higher levels of customer satisfaction, and greater financial success. When employees stay with a company for an extended period, they develop a deep understanding of the organizational structure, culture, and operations. The last thing you want is to invest in six years of training an employee to become an expert, only to have them leave and take that knowledge with them to another company.

While there may be various reasons an employee decides to leave, stepping up to recognize their contributions, respecting their opinions, and valuing their work can make a significant impact. Creating a positive culture that fosters appreciation and opportunity can encourage employees to stay and grow within the company. Not only does this benefit the organization by retaining experienced workers, but it also creates a sense of loyalty and commitment from employees toward the company, making all their training even more beneficial.

Teamwork

Collaboration and collective effort through teamwork are crucial elements for cultivating an environment of mutual respect and effective work relationships among employees. However, teamwork can expose instances where certain individuals are not pulling their weight or contributing effectively to the team. In an academic setting, professors often assign group projects. If one of the group members fails to contribute to the project, it can lead to frustration and resentment among other members who are putting in significant effort to complete the task. This same challenge often manifests itself in a business environment where teamwork is a commonly adopted approach for addressing complex problems and harnessing new opportunities.

To effectively manage this problem, clear rules and expectations must be established so each team member understands their responsibilities and how their efforts contribute to the team's overall success. If a team member is not meeting their expectations, it is a leader's responsibility to address the issue promptly and objectively. Allowing ineffective contributors to remain on the team can hinder the progress of the group as a whole and negatively affect morale.

Since various tasks often impact multiple facets of business operations, it is imperative to assemble a team with members representing each area involved and collectively engage them in the decision-making process. This approach enables the team to identify successful processes and areas requiring improvement. The team can leverage each other's expertise and knowledge to brainstorm and develop novel ideas that will optimize processes.

By working together towards a common goal, team members experience a heightened sense of accomplishment. When leaders promote their employees' sense of accomplishment over time, their hard work can become acknowledged and respected by others.

The bond and camaraderie that develops among team members is an asset that improves the mental and emotional well-being of everyone involved. Happy employees are more engaged, focused, and productive in their work. On the other hand, employees who are unhappy and unmotivated tend to exhibit inferior work habits such as frequent coffee breaks, tardiness, early departure, and lack of productivity. It's important to recognize and develop employees who contribute to a collaborative and supportive work environment because they may have the potential to become strong leaders in the company. We can encourage employees to engage in conversation with their peers during coffee breaks and actively promote the sharing of knowledge and ideas.

Teamwork is the foundation of the curriculum in the United States Military Academy leadership courses, where some service members are multi-functional, and others have a single expertise. In a Special Forces team, each person has a specific skill set that is crucial to the success of the mission. One team member might be an expert in radios, while another might be an expert in local languages. There could also be a topographic expert on the team who can read maps and navigate the team safely. Every person on the team has a specific skill set that contributes to the overall success of the mission, and the team is selected based on the specific mission and the required skill set.

However, people in the Special Forces also possess a variety of skills. They have multiple disciplines they are trained in and also have skills they developed from their experiences. There may be someone who is a small arms expert, but they are also trained as a medic and can operate radios. Someone else may be an expert in M60 machine guns while also being a linguist and an excellent navigator. All of these talents converging is what makes teams successful. When you lose someone on your team, it cripples the success of the rest of the team, and it's impossible to replace them because of how unique their skills are. This is the reason why teams may have a lot of people who share similar skills, especially in the military where they can't risk losing their only sniper expert. Just as in business, when you lose an employee, you lose their expertise which impacts the team, the division, and the company as a whole.

The success of a Special Forces team depends on the collective skills of each team member. They are carefully selected based on their expertise, and together, they can accomplish things that would be impossible for an individual to achieve. Teamwork is critical in the military because it can make the difference between life and death. By bringing together individuals with unique skills and expertise, the team can overcome obstacles and succeed in their mission.

It's not just the military that values the power of teamwork; every other sector does as well because they rely on it to create quality products and deliver quality services to customers. No matter how skilled or talented any individual is, their ability to contribute to a project is limited. They can only work so fast, handle a certain number of tasks, and possess a certain skill set. When you bring together a team with diverse skill sets and complementary strengths, they can accomplish far more than any individual could on their own. Each member brings their unique perspective, expertise, and experience to the table, enlarging the collective knowledge base and enabling the team to overcome challenges and hurdles more quickly.

A team can only achieve its goals if each member is willing to share their ideas, provide constructive feedback, and offer support to their colleagues. Only then can the team move forward together seamlessly and efficiently pushing towards success. Teamwork is critical to the success of any organization, big or small. By building an environment that values collaboration and fosters an atmosphere of mutual support, companies can unleash their collective potential and deliver top-quality results to their clients. So, whether you're in the military, software development, healthcare, or any other industry, teamwork is the key to unlocking your success.

Rise of Upward Management

Over the years, there has been a significant shift in the corporate world – juniors are now managing seniors. This phenomenon is commonly referred to as upward management. In the past, this would have been considered a highly unlikely scenario, but now it is becoming more and more common. Companies are restructuring their organizational hierarchy to be more flexible and adaptable to the changing business landscape. As Boomers are retiring and the younger workforce is rising, this trend can be attributed to several factors, including the growing importance of technical expertise, an emphasis on teamwork and collaboration, and a renewed focus on leadership development. As a result, organizations are more open to promoting individuals who have the right skill set, regardless of their seniority level.

As the younger generation enters the workforce, they often find themselves discussing the challenges of managing their managers. Many managers are stretched thin and under-resourced, leading to frustration and overwhelm among their team members. In such cases, some employees with strong leadership abilities may step up to fill in the gaps left by their managers. But how does one balance their leadership skills with the authority of their manager? It can be a tricky balance to strike, but it is possible with open communication and a strong work ethic.

Upward management doesn't always have to be negative. As a young manager, I was responsible for overseeing many employees who had been working in their positions for decades and had a great deal of knowledge. When employees move on to other positions or retire, we typically lose their wisdom. However, by managing up, they taught me a lot about the work they do and what they have learned over the years. If someone thought I overstepped in speaking to an employee based on their experience within the company and they communicated to me why respectfully, I was then able to take that new knowledge to better our team and the company as a whole.

When it comes to upward management, it's important to strike a balance between respect for their position and being able to assert your ideas and opinions. This might seem like a tricky task, but when done well, it can make for a productive and positive work environment for both parties. It's important to remember your manager is ultimately accountable for the team's success, so your input will carry more weight if it's framed in a way that prioritizes the team's goals. This might mean acknowledging their experience and expertise while still advocating for your own ideas. By showing respect and being willing to listen, you can foster a sense of collaboration and mutual understanding that benefits everyone.

When in a situation of upward management, do not underestimate the importance of cultivating your leadership skills. Even if you are not in a top position, taking the initiative to develop your leadership abilities can greatly benefit your role and your team. Developing leadership skills helps individuals to assume greater responsibilities, work collaboratively with colleagues, and communicate effectively with their supervisors. By dedicating time and effort to honing these skills, you can open new avenues for career growth and more effectively navigate the challenges of managing those in positions of authority. Finding the right balance between your leadership skills and your manager's authority is a crucial aspect of professional growth.

However, this applies to managers who are truly willing to listen. Sometimes, it may not be that easy. Dealing with an incompetent person in a position they shouldn't have been assigned to can be difficult and frustrating. It's understandable to wonder how that employee secured the job in the first place. Although working around their shortcomings may feel overwhelming, it's possible to manage the situation efficiently. Most of the time, they are well aware of their limitations and don't take feedback well. Despite this, it's still possible to succeed in such an environment. To do so, you will have to bring your best game every day and remain focused on achieving your goals despite any obstacles.

Patience is key when dealing with someone who is not up to the task they were given. Instead of arguing with them or discarding their opinion, think about ways to make improvements through collaboration and communication. Without giving up on your own work ethic, actively seek ways to motivate each other towards success and never hesitate to ask for help when needed. For any progress or development to occur, managing an incompetent person has its requirements: persistence, focus, and understanding before anything else. It's easy to become discouraged by how challenging it can be, but remember patience is valuable in situations like these. With determination, it's still possible to reach success even when things don't seem ideal at first glance.

Social and Psychological Aspects

We often have situations that are out of our control, especially in business, and some of those can impact the projects we are working on and our overall delivery. As leaders and managers, it is our responsibility to recognize them early on and make adjustments to divert any obstacles that could be a detriment to the company. When possible, we need to correct the problem or be sympathetic to why it is a problem when we have no control over it.

The most common shifts out of our control are social aspects. Sometimes, customers' needs evolve or change. When we change a product to meet the needs of a growing customer base, it could upset the customers we have been selling to for the last 25 years. You may not have been the person responsible for making the change, but you are responsible for managing that change by explaining the diversification of a product, why you did it, why it's important, and how this change will impact the market. If you care enough about your product, service, and customers, you will make it a point to recognize the effects early on and confront them without ostracizing any particular group of people.

If you are a restaurant owner in NYC, you have to think about all the needs of your potential customers. You may decide to have Kosher options for Jewish customers, meatless options for vegetarians, plant-based options for vegans, and gluten-free options for those with dietary restrictions. Many restaurants across the country are now using symbols on their menu to make it easily identifiable which items contain nuts, meat, dairy, or gluten. This is a great way to meet the growing needs of your customers and show them you care.

These are social aspects we have to adapt to in the management environment because we are working with people who have a variety of backgrounds. When we anticipate and understand the cultural and social needs of our employees, we make it easier to adjust when these arise. When we deliver what employees need to feel holistic in the office, they become more involved in the work they are doing.

As leaders, we also need to be flexible with the psychological aspects of the work environment that may be out of our control. When we think about the education environment in the United States right now, many principals, staff, teachers, and students are in a constant state of stress as a result of the rise of school shootings. As a principal, you need to manage your teachers' emotional well-being to promote a sense of calmness, so their students can feel that calmness as well. You must include the teachers in the process and find out what makes them feel comfortable in their classroom and the school, so the students can feel comfortable as well. We need to be flexible to address the mental and social welfare of our employees because there will always be things happening around us that are out of our control.

So much of our world is changing, and so many bad things are happening. The 5% of bad things override the 95% of good things happening in our environment, and that affects the day-to-day interactions of people and their commitment to their jobs, family, religion, and overall happiness. This is why it's so important to prioritize the social and psychological aspects of our teams. We need to lead with as much understanding as possible and be flexible enough to adapt to the circumstances around us.

THOUGHT MANAGEMENT

- How do the three types of management (downward, upward, and linear) differ from one another?
- Why is training considered a crucial component of any successful business, and in what ways can you diversify the training available to your staff?
- How can teamwork benefit an organization, and what are the challenges associated with managing ineffective team members?
- What is upward management, and what are the factors contributing to its rise in the corporate world? How can one effectively manage upward?

CHAPTER 6

VISION MANAGEMENT

> "The only thing worse than being blind is
> having sight but no vision."
>
> HELEN KELLER

Nothing great can be accomplished without a vision. Think about putting a man on the moon. Do you think Neil Armstrong would have ever planted that flag on the moon if his vision was just to be the first man in space instead of on the moon? The same can be said for any great breakthrough or innovation from the beginning of time. Thomas Edison did not accidentally stumble on the lightbulb; he spent thousands of hours and failed hundreds of times in his quest to replace the candle—not just make a better version of the candle. This is exactly how great leaders approach business.

Good managers can keep a team aligned with the company vision, but it takes a leader to define that vision and convey it to their followers.

To effectively accomplish this there are a series of steps involved, all of which I have used within my organizations to motivate teams behind a cause. It is a balancing act of internal standards and external influences. Management can design and implement the checkpoints needed to maintain this balance, but once again must take their cues from leadership. Let's get into the four main areas where you can either execute your vision or muddy the waters for everyone involved.

Mission and Standards

Every company needs to have a detailed mission statement outlining where they have been, where they are going, and what the ultimate destination is. Conforming to that mission statement is all about the process you set up for your employees to participate in it. The roles they play will allow you to accomplish your mission successfully, so you need to establish uniform standards for holding everyone accountable while also giving them the tools to be successful in delivering on that mission.

Leaders need to ensure the missions and standards align with and enhance the vision. Always think of your vision as the outcome or the end product of your missions. You may have a few small visions you are looking to accomplish to achieve the overall vision. There are interlocking aspects of the mission to make up the vision, and all of those aspects need to be managed accordingly. The missions should be tailored and catered to in such a way that they are all-encompassing rather than fragmented based on departments or teams. They have to come together as a whole to have a successful and implementable vision.

Missions could include:

- Employee buy-in
- Compliance
- Manager acceptance

Vision management is the responsibility of the leader. Each mission should be properly communicated to the team implementing it and have a point person in charge to ensure everyone pulls together to execute their mission. Each point person is then responsible for ensuring compliance with standards, determining what feedback is viable, and when something is out of the scope of their mission. One of the hardest concepts in vision management is when employees get off track and go on tangents without any sound footing. They may spend weeks or months working on something that comes to a crashing halt once they discover it or someone else informs them it no longer applies or is not in compliance with the missions at hand. Although they may have the best intentions, it doesn't deliver anything tangible to the outcome, which is the vision. If the vision is not tangible enough for people to put in their pockets and walk around with it, it's not going to be something they work toward daily.

In our personal charitable foundation, our vision is to turn the Helm Foundation into a household name for those who are looking to give back to their community. Within that, there are three different missions we are focusing on based on the subset of people who can donate money, and we have developed a marketing plan for each of these including individual giving, small corporations, and churches. If our mission is to provide a new pair of sneakers for every person experiencing homelessness, then we would work closely with a shoe manufacturer on the small corporation side to have them donate shoes and partner with a church that can then reach those experiencing homelessness and have a point location to distribute the shoes while we recruit volunteers to hand them out.

While our overall vision may be broad, the individual missions necessary for bringing that vision to life are all designed in a way that 100% of donations are guaranteed to go to the grassroots of the people who need help because I personally cover all the overhead expenses for the foundation. Many organizations spend a large percentage of their funding on operation costs to pay the people who run the organization, but we cover those expenses personally, which aligns with our vision of enabling the Helm Foundation to have the greatest impact possible.

You want to live by and create according to your mission statement, so you need to create standards to ensure you stay on target. If you have a mission statement to provide a new backpack to every student experiencing homelessness in Detroit, you need to have the best process for identifying students who are experiencing homelessness, access to quality backpacks of varying sizes, and the ability to reach those students by complying with the guidelines of the school and shelters systems. Mission statements without borders, parameters, and the ability to adjust to the changing environment are useless and can be more problematic than not having a mission statement at all.

External Mandates and Requirements

Every company that produces anything must conform to external requirements and mandates. If you own a deli, you are required to follow guidelines from the Food and Drug Administration. Automobile manufacturers have to meet different state and federal requirements for emissions. Banks and other financial service institutions have to be aware of anti-discrimination and consumer protection laws. There are a variety of different agencies depending on the type of business, and some of those agencies may perform audits to ensure compliance in those areas. Under-conforming to these external mandates and requirements can be detrimental to a company.

External mandates can come from outside agencies or even other departments inside a company. Quality control has its own set of compliance requirements that other departments need to align with. Quality control's job is to maintain the standards to ensure a product or service is successful and customers can fully reap the benefits of utilizing it.

One of the most difficult aspects of dealing with external requirements is they are always changing. Some may only change periodically, but others might change daily, such as the policies during COVID, which were dictated by both federal and state compliance as well as industry-specific requirements. This is why it's incredibly important for leaders to understand all the requirements they are dealing with and the pace at which they change in the industry.

Quality and Conformity of Work Product Over Time

When you have a product or service, quality control is a major part of your business. A quality product is more than just conforming to a standard. It is the life breath of your company and causes your company to exist. It's knowing there is a consumer who needs this, or else you wouldn't be in business to begin with. Because of this, quality control and internal compliance are vital to your business. If you find one day that you didn't do something right, you need to come up with a plan to fix it and make it quicker, better, and faster, so you can continue serving your consumers and being a company that employs people and produces a product people want to purchase many years from now.

Whether you are in banking or manufacturing, your quality assurance process should be immediate, consistent, and performed often. If you miss a measurement or something critical, even by a millimeter, it can cause the product to fail and become unusable. There are quality controls and quality control assurance to help you guarantee the measurements are correct so they will fit the end product down the road. If you are working in pharmaceuticals, you have to do a sampling of the drug to make sure the mixture of the drug is the same as the drug that was tested because that is the drug you were approved to sell. You produced it, tested it, and analyzed its performance. If you aren't keeping the consistency of the drug the same and begin diluting it with other, possibly cheaper ingredients, then you are going to have a major problem with both the Federal Drug Administration and your consumers should they discover the difference in the end product. This is why it's critical to have a process in place where you can check and double-check your product.

In an automobile manufacturing company, there are hundreds, if not thousands, of quality control checks being done along the way to ensure the car can perform at the required level for safety compliance and consumer satisfaction. It could be something as simple as making the hoods for a car. They have to be made with the exact measurements and installed in the exact way. This is one of those products where every millimeter matters because there could be a real gap in production, which could impact the safety of the driver in a fender-bender. At the same time, if you create a braking mechanism for a car, there is a requirement for a certain number of pounds per foot to stop the car. The same five-foot, 100-pound woman should be able to stop a car with the same amount of pressure as a six-foot, 200-pound man.

These are the standards that make all the difference in the world between competitors. There are many different steps, and they may vary depending on the complexity of the product. The more complex a product is, the more quality control standard steps and evaluations will be required during the production cycle. It doesn't have to be manufacturing; this could apply to writing and editing a book as well. The more chapters, sections, and references added to a book, the more you need someone to check and double-check for consistency across the board. There needs to be a process for everything. Every minute of every day counts when your company's reputation is on the line and put to the test. It only takes one failed product or service to ruin a company. These processes are designed to minimize the chances of a product failing and ruining your company's business operations.

Another great example is the Titan Submersible, which was basically operated with a game console controller in the Submersible. I doubt many of us would get on a plane controlled by a pilot who stuck his hand out the window to measure the air pressure and how fast the wind travels. As a consumer, you want to know there are quality control standards in place and conformity to those standards because it gives you confidence in a product. As a company, you want your employees to have the highest level of quality possible for your consumer.

Your standard is your standard—you create it and can form it into whatever you want, but there will always be external mandates and requirements for the bare minimum level of what you are expected to do. The external standard is the minimum standard, but you should be setting your standards to satisfy the highest-level consumer and deliver them the highest-quality product or service.

Employee Compliance

Employee compliance is not so much about the employee showing up to work at 8 a.m. and leaving at 4 p.m., taking only 45-minute lunch breaks, and having two 15-minute breaks each day. It's about learning to lock their computers when they leave the office, meeting deadlines for tasks and projects, and making sure they are communicating any issues or potential problems regarding what is being asked of them. That interactive exchange between employees ensures everyone is staying on target.

Leaders can encourage their peers and employees to adjust to what they didn't accomplish that day and build a bridge to cross any damage that has been done to stay on track in the future. There is also a functional aspect to employee compliance like buy-in, self-assessment, vision adjustment, and mission accomplishment.

The buy-in process is an energy process because it's an exchange between the leaders, managers, and employees to assess what the job is, communicate that, and accomplish the job at hand. It's the employee's responsibility to buy in and take their job seriously to complete the task. When a leader lets someone go, it's usually because they don't do this effectively.

The employee needs to look at what's laid out before them and understand it. They need to analyze what's been communicated to them by their leader or manager and determine what's been said or asked of them. Then, they need to determine if they've done this before or if this is something new they need to learn to do effectively. Lastly, they need to determine if they've been successful at this or something similar to this before. Once they do those three things and talk it out with themselves or someone on their team, they can determine if they want to be an integral part of a company, program, or initiative. If they determine they want to be a part of something, they will then buy in and discover how they can be part of this team to make sure they accomplish what they're working on.

Once the employee is committed, they need to participate in the process, make it better, and help to accomplish the goal. This is where their self-assessment comes into play. If they've done this before and learned from their mistakes, they can get it done quicker, better, and faster. They will look at how they can utilize those learnings from the past to do a better job in the present and in the future. They may need to make major adjustments or minor fine-tunings based on the judgment of what they're dealing with. Their personal self-assessment also helps to solidify the buy-in process because they are actively looking for ways to improve toward the goal.

Vision adjustment may be the hardest but the most obvious part of employee compliance. Everyone involved in the process needs to feel like they're part of the process. If you have a leader who puts the vision out there but fails to listen to constructive feedback from the management team or employees who are accomplishing the process to have successful mission implementation, then the entire team is going to fail. This part is where it's essential for employees to be able to communicate back and forth between their managers and leaders. Just as leaders need to communicate down through the ranks, employees need to communicate up through them. As a leader, you can encourage your managers to listen to what everyone has to say, document it, and discuss it in team meetings. Only then will you see a consensus approach to your vision.

The last part is mission accomplishment. There is no better feeling than watching the rocket ship take off after years spent designing and testing it. The successful launch of any company or vision is one of the best ways a leader can develop and encourage employee compliance. By sharing in the successes, employees will continue to want to be involved in the future because they will feel the same pride in accomplishing the mission that you do. Sharing recognition with your team helps to build self-esteem and pride among your employees.

THOUGHT MANAGEMENT

- Why is having a clear vision essential for accomplishing great breakthroughs or innovations in business, and how do great leaders approach this?

- What are the four main areas involved in vision management, and how do they contribute to executing the vision successfully?

- How can leaders ensure that missions and standards align with and enhance the overall vision, and why is it crucial for missions to be all-encompassing rather than fragmented based on departments or teams?

- What are the challenges associated with external mandates and requirements, and why is it vital for leaders to stay informed about the changing external requirements in their industry?

CHAPTER 7

NAVIGATING THE RUTS OF BUSINESS

"Obstacles are those frightful things you see when you take your eyes off your goal."

HENRY FORD

Many businesses often fail to discuss the management rut. When I talk about the management rut, I like to equate it to a person walking on railroad tracks. They step on the wood planks in between the rails and walk at a comfortable pace. They're following the direction of the tracks, looking down, and not seeing much in front of them or anything to the side of them outside of the rails. By doing that, they don't have the vision to look at the various factors that could be affecting what they're doing. If they're not looking at the sky, they won't know if it's going to rain. If they don't look behind them, they might not know a train is coming. When they're walking within the railroad tracks, they are in a rut because they're not looking at anything other than what's right in front of them.

Complacency is one of the most detrimental things to the overall success of a company. If you get into a habit or a rut, it impacts your overall functionality on the job and the productivity of others. If you are not taking the time to move outside the rails of the railroad tracks to talk to people, understand their concerns, and work for the betterment of the company, you are not going to be an effective manager or leader.

Too many times, people are oblivious to the reality that surrounds them. If you're walking down the railroad tracks and hear a sound in the distance, you need to choose between staying on the tracks or getting off before the train hits you. The sound of the train coming is your wake-up call, but it's up to you to decide what to do next. Sometimes, we get so focused on something that we develop tunnel vision and miss the obvious. Pay attention and be observant of the details around you. You can't navigate around the management rut unless you can admit it's happening, understand it, and take steps to get back on track so you can self-actualize.

The two most important factors in navigating the management rut are assessment and communication. As we assess, leaders need to ask the appropriate questions:

- What's going on here?
- In what ways is it having an impact?
- Why are we not performing at the level we thought we were going to be performing?

- Why was this not brought to the right people's attention to focus on?

- How are we going to ensure this does not happen again?

These questions are important to reflect upon during your self-assessment. We need to ask these questions at every level from employees to supervisors, management, and senior leadership. We are going to look at how each of these plays into the management rut from the perspectives of the managers, the employees, and ourselves.

Manager Rut

While we often think of our lower-level employees getting into a rut, it's important to be aware managers can easily fall into the management rut as well. If you walk through a department at 5:02 p.m. and notice none of the managers are there, or they're there but not engaging with the employees, it's likely there is a management rut. When a manager isn't walking around, talking to employees, and soliciting ideas from them, this prevents the company from improving. Not only will the managers stop caring, but the employees will as well because they set the example.

When a manager is away on vacation, I like to pay particular attention to their department, check-in, and see how they are doing. You can tell a lot about a manager based on the way their department responds when they aren't around. Communication with that department allows you to assess what they are working on, how well it is going, and if you notice any hurdles. If an employee in a department makes a mistake and tells you the manager has never corrected them for that, it means you need to check in with the manager when they get back to see if it's something they were unaware of or if they simply don't care because they are in a management rut.

One of the most difficult tasks of a leader is keeping management engaged in what they're doing and making sure they share the goals and aspirations of the company. We often find there are a lot of managers who have simply grown into a position because they have been with a company for an extended period. They may not necessarily have the experience or skills to be successful in management, but they have taken on more responsibilities over time and got the title of manager. These are often the managers you need to watch because they are more likely to disengage and fall into a management rut.

It's a shame when an employee who has been on board for six weeks informs the manager of a major problem they should have known about earlier. You can't possibly know everything though. Even the most seasoned managers can have this happen to them in their departments because we sometimes need an outside perspective to see these issues. Good leaders try to prevent this though by having regular meetings with their teams to discuss obstacles and stay on top of any potential future issues.

A leader can prevent themselves and their teams from getting into a management rut through effective communication and assessments. Managers should not be exempt from performance reviews simply because they are managers. Their performance reviews are essential to ensure they are not in a management rut. If you don't communicate with managers about what is going on, you can't expect them to change their behavior or mentality. You need to provide them with that information and develop a program or process for assessment and communication.

Employee Rut

As a leader or manager, you're likely very familiar with this rut because we see it most often with employees who come to work, punch in 30 seconds before their shift starts, and then stand at the time clock and wait to punch out at the end of the day. They don't want to work overtime or do anything more than is expected of them. But before you can coach them out of this rut, you have to communicate with them, assess their performance, and then communicate with them again to share where they need to make improvements. When you communicate with them, it's important to have a discussion where you can create a plan of action with their input rather than simply direct them on what they need to do.

If you have an employee whose shift ends at 5 p.m., but they are rushing out of the office at 4:45 p.m. every day, your job is to communicate what you are observing and ask about it. By approaching them in a conversation and saying, "I noticed you often rush to be in your car by 4:45 p.m. to leave for the day. Is there something going on that's causing you to rush out of here, and is there anything I can do to help?"

You might find out they simply need to pick up their child from daycare no later than 5 p.m. or they are trying to make it to their child's baseball practice twice each week. These are very common situations for employees that can be easily solved with basic communication. It might involve adjusting work times or simply allowing that 15-minute grace period if they are a high-performing member of the team and completing their tasks regularly and on time. The latter would require some assessment to ensure they are completing their work effectively and efficiently.

If you communicate with them and they have no explanation for the behavior, it's a good time to do an assessment. In the assessment, you may also notice they are missing deadlines or are getting bad customer ratings. All of this evidence is a sign of a rut. You can ask the questions at the beginning of this chapter, address any issues at their performance review, and come to an agreement on how to best solve the challenges together.

However, if you assess them and discover they are completing more than their assigned work, this is where your discretion as a manager comes into play. You may decide rushing out at the end of the day is fine because they are still going above and beyond. However, as a word of caution, be careful to not show favoritism. Ask yourself if you'd give other employees the same leniency and communicate to your team how they can get the same perk. You can ask this employee if they are still feeling challenged by their work. This allows you to help them with their professional development. If you find they are underperforming during your assessment, this is absolutely something to address with the employee so you can provide them with the opportunity to adjust their behavior.

Another way to recognize an employee rut is if you discover no one on the team is actively communicating the existing problems with the manager. Managers shouldn't always have to figure out what's wrong. If team members aren't communicating, it could be that the team is in a rut or feels their manager is in a rut. If there is a problem and the team is not making you aware of it, this is something that can be included in their goals and aspirations during their performance reviews. Doing this allows the employees to identify where they are and where they need to be. By communicating this with them, they can make the necessary changes to get out of this rut.

If you are effectively communicating with all levels and continue to do self-assessments to try to identify potential problems, you can establish a culture of continuous improvement where a management rut is not acceptable. When we are observing what should be done differently, it all boils down to communication. If you don't give instructions or your assessment of the situation, you will end up perpetuating the rut for your employees. A lot of managers will say they're too busy to talk to an employee about what's going on, but if they fail to get to the root of the problem, the employee will never reach their full potential.

It's like a car driving through an intersection without paying attention to the other cars on the road. Unfortunately, many people who have been in a real rut on the side of the road may spin their wheels, but the wheels only drag them deeper and deeper into the mud because they need support to get out of their rut. They need someone to help them, and that's the job of the manager or leader. Only once we help employees can they reach their full potential, which allows the company to reach its full potential.

Keep in mind, the employees who are working during their 15-minute breaks in the office are those who know they need to work on something or fix something. Those employees are the superstars you want on your team. Because they are putting in extra effort to get something done rather than put it off until later. These employees have the mindset necessary to drive the company forward when it's necessary to get something done. They even work on or support projects that are outside of the scope of their job when it doesn't give them any monetary gains. They're not working overtime just to make some extra money; they're working because they believe in what the company is trying to accomplish and want to play a key role in that.

It's worth mentioning though that requiring or expecting employees to work through their breaks or work overtime as part of your culture can be very dangerous and cause employee burnout. Your employees are entitled to their breaks, so if you notice one or all of your employees working through their breaks, there may be larger issues in the company in terms of culture or workflow. It could be the process, a lack of skills or knowledge on a team, or anything in between. Be careful this doesn't become the norm because employees will be bound to get into a rut. Everyone needs downtime to disengage from work so they can come back with a fresh view of things.

There are management types out there who see themselves as people who make things happen rather than supporting the work as their team goes along. Employees need to be recognized and rewarded for their extra effort. This could be as simple as saying something positive about their work effort, which goes a long way toward boosting employee self-esteem and morale. We often underestimate how taking employees for granted can leave them in a rut, so always make sure to encourage them and give them a boost when you can. If they're against a deadline, be a leader by showing them support and helping them to meet that deadline. Most importantly, always say thank you.

Self Rut

If you are the person experiencing the rut, it can be more challenging to identify. The management rut is a state of mind, which means we might simply not see it. When we don't recognize it as a problem, we won't want to do anything about it. In any management situation, it's easy for people to simply say, "Oh, this is just a normal bump we run into."

This is why continuous self-assessment is important. You need to figure out what is causing this rut and how you can fix it to be more supportive of the company overall. Whether you are aware you are off-track or not, self-assess periodically using the questions at the beginning of this chapter to avoid getting stuck in a rut. Ask yourself:

- What's going on here?
- In what ways is it having an impact?
- Why am I not performing at the level I thought I was going to be performing?
- Why is this not brought to the right people's attention to focus on?
- How are we going to ensure this does not happen again?

In addition to self-assessment, you should be communicating with your team and anyone you report to directly to get their feedback and input. They may be able to give you a new perspective you did not see otherwise. The success of any employee, manager, or leader is more dependent upon self-assessment in their work environment than any other type of assessment. Too many individuals have a prima-donna attitude that they can do no wrong and fail to look at themselves critically, specifically when it comes to the way they lead. Continuous self-assessment is the greatest tool we are given as individuals, and it goes underutilized. There are so many books out there on self-assessment, so pick up any of them to start your self-development.

Oftentimes, we can find ourselves in a rut when we aren't being challenged enough. As humans, we favor what's familiar to us, but it often prevents us from self-actualizing. This is especially true in our careers. If we don't feel challenged, we lack the motivation to take on new challenges. There are a lot of ways to jumpstart your performance, and it starts by not brushing it under the rug and thinking it will take care of itself. Management ruts can become major hurdles in our personal and professional lives and have negative impacts on our company at large.

Once you recognize you're in a rut, you need to focus on getting out of it. Sometimes, the best thing you can do is stop everything and assess what is happening before you move forward. If you're in a hole, you might just be digging yourself deeper and deeper while continuing to go about your daily activities. Once you perform a self-assessment, you should communicate with the team to gather facts. Then, you can lay out a game plan to execute any new policies, procedures, or changes you are going to make. You will need to communicate all of these changes to everyone involved for them to be effective. Then, you can assess again to see if you are working your way out of the rut or if you still need to make additional changes. If you're back on track, you just need to make sure you don't slip back into old habits.

Too many times in management, we fix something but fail to account for other complications that have arisen as a result of the fix we implemented. Other complications could be:

- Loss of enthusiasm
- Lack of teamwork
- Lack of attention to detail
- Decrease in feedback
- Lack of self-assessment or evaluation
- Harm to culture, environment, and company

If you don't take care of these issues and address them holistically, they are going to impact your products and services and your business overall. When we are better managers, it can transform other areas of our lives as well. We become better parents, better spouses, and better friends because we strive to be the best we can be in every situation.

THOUGHT MANAGEMENT

- Why is complacency detrimental to a company's success?

- How can leaders use assessment and communication, as the two most important factors in navigating the management rut, to identify and address issues?

- How can managers fall into the management rut, and what are the signs that indicate a manager may be disengaged from their team?

- Why is continuous self-assessment crucial for personal and professional development?

CHAPTER 8

SET THE EXAMPLE

"Setting an example is not the main means of
influencing others; it is the only means."

ALBERT EINSTEIN

When you're in a management position, whether it's a supervisor, manager, or executive leader, you need to set an example. When other people look up to you and see you have the right kind of dedication to do the job and be involved in the company, they will follow suit. Likewise, if they see you are not doing what is expected of you, they are going to go in whatever direction they see fit.

Setting the example is not a singular event. It's a massive, ongoing initiative. It can only be viewed as successful when the masses follow the protocol to be the best they can be. It's hard to set the protocol for the masses if it's not being executed at the top level. This is something I have always looked for when setting up my leadership team because

I understand everyone else will be looking at them to set an example. When you have people who set the example and instill that in their direct reports, you create an overall level of employee satisfaction within your company, a company of doers instead of observers, and a work environment based on camaraderie.

In the military, we had slackers, the soldiers who did their job 100% but nothing more, and the soldiers who went beyond the call of duty. In those environments, the first thing you notice is that the slackers stay together. If you're a slacker, you know who the other slackers are. If you're someone who does a great job, you recognize the others who do a good job as well, and you may even aspire to do better. One of the hardest things to do is transform a slacker into an overachiever without being critical of them. You have to provide constructive criticism in a way that is direct but also sensitive to where they are currently at in their professional development and personal life. This feedback provides them with the awareness and education they need to be productive. However, before we can correct the weaknesses in others, we need to correct the weaknesses within ourselves as a way of setting an example for others to follow. No one is perfect, and if you try to convince people you are, then you're not setting the example of a successful leader.

Unhappy people don't produce a good product. If you set an example, you can create a much better culture for your employees, which will make them want to do a better job. They will take pride in what they do and want to do better.

Dedication

We all know of someone, in our company or not, who simply works to get a paycheck, but your responsibility as a leader is to show your dedication. A leader's dedication sets an example for their team and others in the organization to follow. How you do the job and how much pride you take in your work inspires others to go the extra mile too. If you lack dedication, how can you expect others to be dedicated? It's not just dedication to making profits, but dedication to quality products and services, workers' rights, treating people equitably, and showing people they are appreciated.

Dedication is one of the more ambiguous elements to evaluate. While blatant dedication stands out, a lot of dedicated employees may fly under the radar. Not everyone will be extremely dedicated, but you want to reinforce dedication through a process of appreciation and acknowledgment over a period of time to see how individuals commit to the overall success of your company. This then sets the example for other employees and managers as well. Dedication is infectious. When you have some departments where everyone is very dedicated, other people will pick that up. Unfortunately, you may find some imposters who want to ride the wave of dedication from everyone else, but they aren't truly dedicated to the mission or the company.

In a business environment, there needs to be expectations that everyone is equally dedicated and contributes to the overall success of the company. They all need to buy into the process at each level, from employees to managers to senior leadership. When dedication exists on all levels, it provides for seamlessness across the organization where everyone contributes equally regardless of their rank within the company.

Recognition & Awards

It's important for a manager to recognize people on their team. If you recognize individuals and groups for the good job they do, then they are going to recognize the people who work for them. Then, they will also report on that to their department heads. Recognition doesn't always have to be about money. It can come through communication or a pat on the back.

Another way to give recognition is through rewards. You can give someone money as an award, but you can also award them with "Employee of the Month" or another similar award such as "Highest Sales of the Month." These awards don't cost the company anything other than a piece of paper. You can also give them a prize. For instance, if they figured out a way for your department to save $200 per month, you can offer them a gift card for dinner for two at a local restaurant. When employees do exceptional things, they should be exceptionally rewarded.

If a whole team performs well, you could award them with a luncheon or a team outing. You could also award them with an additional paid day off and turn a three-day weekend into four days. This may not cost you money directly, but time is something everyone values.

Involvement & Inclusivity

People like to be involved because it gives them a sense of belonging. If you have a meeting to discuss what you're doing in the company, invite people to join in. If someone is interested in learning a skill or moving into another department, you can allow them to shadow someone in another department. Find out what your employees feel is missing from their work experience to feel fulfilled and try to fill those gaps when possible. This should be done at all levels from employees to supervisors and from managers to the leadership team. Cross-pollination between departments signifies all departments are aligned and working together to achieve their goals.

When you do this, make sure you are giving these opportunities to the people who are right for them. If Jason is an engineer and doesn't express interest or have the skills to understand financing, it's not in anyone's best interest to move him to the accounting department just because you need to fill a position there. We don't want to move employees around just because we feel like we need to or because we need to meet quotas. This is the worst possible thing you could do as a leader. However, if you think someone would be great in another department or could excel professionally from learning in other departments, you should always offer them the opportunity to do so.

Every time we acquired another company or function, I would set up a two-hour meeting with all of my direct reports and give them as much detail about the acquisition as I could without breaking any confidentiality rules. When you're a public company, you don't want that information getting out to your people before you tell them. Sharing this information and letting them know how sensitive the information is will allow them to feel involved in the transition that is happening.

It's important to understand the pluses and minuses that go along with the mission while also being sensitive to the fact that you are dealing with all the people and aspects that go into it. This is a good time to take a step back and be aware of whether it would be more beneficial or detrimental to the company to involve certain levels within the organization. This is where a leader's discretion and decision-making become important.

Collaboration

As a leader, you are responsible for setting an example when it comes to collaboration. Whether it's members of your team or multiple departments working together to complete a process or goal, you need to show employees what is expected of them in these scenarios. You can do this by recognizing each individual as a critical part of the organization and making sure they are part of the process. By setting the stage for this, you open up the door for full collaboration among your teams, showing you are also a team player who is open to participating and receiving feedback on the process.

Collaboration is about interfacing with the individual you are in parallel with and the people you cross over in your everyday work. The way you behave and interact with others will signal to your team what is "appropriate" for them to do and say in these collaborative environments. If you want your team to work effectively with other teams, you must be open to collaborating with other teams and other departments and show how you want them to act so the company can work together as a whole. If you are a manager and you tell your team you don't like Sally from the accounting department, chances are, your team won't like her either and will refuse to collaborate with Sally or members of her team toward a common goal. Sometimes, this requires putting aside your personal feelings and showing up professionally for the sake of the success of the company.

The quickest way to fail is by making decisions in a vacuum. You have to always take your team into account, listen to what they have to say, and truly take their feedback. If you decide to take action without getting collaborative feedback from your team or the people around you, it becomes more difficult to get buy-in and makes it easier for them to blame you if something goes wrong or fails altogether. It's not about making other people part of the problem, but when you work together, it shows you tried to work toward a common goal and got all the necessary feedback and support you could to be successful.

It's one thing for the leadership or management level to set the example, and it's another for them to show those on all levels how to set the example. Part of what we want to teach people who work for us is how to get comfortable with who they are and what they are capable of so they can set an example for other members of our organization as well.

I've been in work environments where we had employees who didn't feel their supervisor was contributing what they should have at the level for which they were being compensated. That's not setting a positive example because it can quickly perpetuate down the line, causing other employees to slack off as well. We focus mostly on the leader because it is a snowball effect from there, but it could start from anyone within the organization. When we fail to set an example, we leave things open for interpretation and allow bad habits to become part of the culture of the company. This is why leaders at all levels need to set an example and ensure the example is being followed by team members.

THOUGHT MANAGEMENT

- Why is it important for managers and leaders to set an example in the workplace?

- What are some ways leaders can demonstrate dedication to their work and the company, and how does this influence employee behavior?

- How can recognition and awards be used as effective tools for motivating and inspiring employees?

- What role does collaboration play in leadership, and how can leaders foster a collaborative culture within their teams and across different departments?

CONCLUSION

*"Excellent leaders navigate past the roadblocks
to successfully complete their journey."*

H. MARC HELM

Being a leader is not easy. If it was, everyone would be doing it, and there would be no followers. At face value, that sounds like it could be a good thing. We have assigned a negative connotation to being a "follower," but the truth of the matter is that the world needs followers. Just like we cannot have a society without doctors and ditch diggers, military officers and religious zealots, or teachers and students, we cannot have leaders without followers. But more importantly, we cannot have followers without leaders. Can you imagine what the world would be like if everyone was just standing around waiting for someone to take the lead, only for that person to never show up?

Even though being a leader is difficult, it is not impossible. The steps and principles outlined in this book should get you started on the right path in your never-ending leadership journey. That's right—leadership is a journey, not a destination. There is not a leader on Earth who has it all figured out, accomplished everything they want to, and is ready to sit back and hand over the reins. Why do you think some of our most noteworthy leaders such as Warren Buffet, Oprah Winfrey, Mark Zuckerberg, and others are continuously improving? They have accumulated more wealth than any one person can spend in a lifetime, possibly several lifetimes, but they still wake up every day with the plan of innovating and leading their teams through whatever turbulent waters may arise.

Here's the thing, though—no one told either of these people they had to be leaders. This was a decision they consciously made and then took the necessary steps to make that dream become a reality. The same will be true on your journey. But considering you picked up this book, and I assume you finished it if you are now reading this, you have taken the first step onto the path. There will be ups and downs, times to celebrate, and times when you might want to quit. As long as you recognize that upfront, the low points won't feel so bad or come as much of a surprise, and the good moments will be that much sweeter.

I would suggest the following:

- If you have read this book, read it again.
- Use a highlighter to highlight anything you want to remember or tag the pages.

- Over time in management, refer back to the book and make notations of anything you tried and how it worked for you.

- When you are done with the book, pass it on to someone else.

HAPPY LEADING!

ABOUT THE AUTHOR

H. Marc Helm's narrative defies the ordinary, weaving a story that intertwines resilience, unconventional choices, and a wealth of experience.

Emanating from modest roots and shaped by the crucible of the Vietnam War, he found purpose during nearly seven years of U.S. Army service, which propelled him toward academic achievements in sociology and psychology, both accomplished with Honors.

After departing from the predictable trajectory of finance, Marc's unorthodox path led him to explore executive coaching and consulting, realms where his multidisciplinary insights flourish, guiding individuals and organizations through uncharted territories.

In this fusion of diverse pursuits, Marc embodies a modern Renaissance spirit, amplified by over forty-six years of financial services, mortgage banking, and entrepreneurial experience, proving that success is as much about embracing the extraordinary as it is about adhering to conventions.

www.ingramcontent.com/pod-product-compliance
Lightning Source LLC
Chambersburg PA
CBHW020847210326
41597CB00041B/1036